DUMB BUNNIES
and
EXPECTING CATS

THANKS FOR YOUR SUPPORT OF THE HUMANE SOCIETY WITH PURCHASE OF THIS BOOK!

Matthew C. Moen

2014

DUMB BUNNIES
and
EXPECTING CATS

MATTHEW C. MOEN

FRODE BOOKS

ISBN: 978-0-9899365-2-1
LCCN: PENDING

Cover Design by Angela Gier
Editing by Josette Haddad
Typeset by Biz Cook

Printed in the United States of America

MATTHEW C. MOEN   FRODE BOOKS

Dedicated to Donna Lynn Moen,
wife, cat lover, caregiver

And to Erika Lynn Moen,
daughter, cat lover, aspiring author

TABLE OF CONTENTS

Preface

THIS STORY WAS WRITTEN in a timely manner but was then squirreled away in a desk drawer for a very long time because a young professor striving to earn the respect of the community of scholars does not lightly publish a cat book.

But things change.

Enough serious scholarship has appeared with my name on it that colleagues will be amused to learn of my foray into the world of creative nonfiction. And turning fifty changes one's personal calculations. Benefits in the fifties include accumulated wisdom, financial security, and a full ten percent off hotels through AARP. But bubbling around in every man's head during his sixth decade of life is cramming in some new ventures because he has already climbed so many rungs of the ladder of life, without knowing the precise distance to the top. The generally proper ladies of the community use the same thought process when they don red hats and purple dresses.

I also hope this undertaking teaches my daughter some helpful lessons. Erika was not yet born when this book was first written, but she began writing all on her own early in life—poetry, a novella, and a short essay in a book of stories published by the South Dakota Humanities Council. In fact, her birthday was my inspiration to retrieve this story from the desk drawer and put some final touches on it; I surprised her with a manuscript that she had no idea even existed. Subsequently, she offered some humorous and thoughtful tweaks.

My wife, Donna, is a kind-hearted person and the quintessential cat lover. She has done so much for so many helpless cats over the years, patiently nursing them back to health and finding them proper homes. She deserves thanks for encouraging me to write this story, while always accepting her part in it with gracious good humor. That is also true for my parents, Kenneth and Verona Moen.

Many cats have roamed into my life. In fact, my wife and daughter welcome them into our home on a regular basis. A basement playhouse originally built for kids was converted to shelter abandoned and stray cats. And we've housed all manner of felines—cats in ones and twos, entire litters of kittens, injured and healthy adult cats, and feral cats tamed into household pets. We've had fancy cats, stray cats, brown cats, wounded cats, black cats, rowdy cats, calico cats, and cats that did not make it.

We've been involved with antibiotics, kitten formula, bottle-feeding, Elizabethan collars, and euthanasia. Right now we have a feral ruffian turned fat and happy house cat; we also adopted a waif from the Singing Hills Animal Hospital in nearby Sioux City, Iowa, who cannot believe his good fortune at landing in a home where my wife and daughter grasp his needs even before he thinks them up.

Readers seeking an understanding of some of the lesser-known elements of feline behavior as part of an offbeat cat tale have come to the right place.

I wish to thank some friends who are genuine book lovers. Sherry DeBoer, Lynn Rognstad, Ann McKay Thompson, and Judy Zwolak all read the manuscript and encouraged me to push ahead. Angela Gier designed a fetching cover, while Josette Haddad did a great job of copyediting. Finally, I'm grateful to several faculty in a first-rate Department of English at the University of South Dakota, including Brian Bedard, Emily Haddad, and especially Lee Ann Roripaugh, who facilitated my first public reading at the 2013 John R. Milton Writer's Conference.

And now, after suppressing this story for years, it's time to sally forth, all the while mischievously smiling to myself at the thought of any naysayers out there who are watching my climb up the ladder of life in the male equivalent of a red hat and purple dress.

It can't be a pleasant sight.

1

Gratitude Is Not a Strong Suit of Cats

WHO EVER HEARD OF a cat requiring a cesarean section? I stared blankly at the phone for a second and then asked the veterinarian whether a C-section was really necessary. But I only vaguely listened to his reply, already wondering how I was going to pay for the operation on my paltry graduate-student stipend. Major abdominal surgery for felines was hardly a budgeted item.

Ever anxious to save a buck, I reentered the conversation and asked the same question a different way.

"Are you really sure that she won't deliver by herself?" I inquired, shuffling my feet nervously at the inevitable answer. "I mean, don't cats usually get this done by themselves?"

"Well, yes, they usually do," the vet replied. But it wasn't going to happen this time.

Of the more than fifty million cats in the United States in the mid-1980s, I happened to draw the hard-luck cat from the infinitesimal pool of pregnant felines that needed surgical assistance to deliver kittens. Talk about drawing the shortest of short straws.

This looming financial fiasco was downright surreal to a twenty-seven-year-old who had grown up in South Dakota, where I was taught to think about animals mostly in terms of very fat cows and pigs as a ticket to prosperity, not in terms of emergency surgery for distressed momma kitty cats. After all, South Dakota is a state where the occasional character erects a billboard on his own farmland gleefully pointing out that animal rights activism interferes with making a good living. It is a place where kids tenderly raise farm animals through their local 4-H clubs to win blue ribbons at county fairs, and then sometimes turn around and butcher them. Paying out of my meager bank account to save one lone kitty that had only recently come into my life had never been part of my life plan.

As the obligatory conversation with the veterinarian dragged on and gradually turned toward a more detailed description of the envisioned surgical process, my thoughts began to drift further and further away from the matter at hand. This is explained by simple manners. Midwestern boys are taught early on, or else are wise enough to figure out all on their own, that it is generally quite rude to discuss female gynecological issues over the telephone, especially with complete strangers.

East and West Coast people may think that life is all one dang reality television show, but those of us in the heartland know better than gratuitously discussing the sensitive topic of the female reproductive system. Proof is that we remain suspicious of teaching kids in public schools about human anatomy, even when they are segregated by gender.

A lot of crazy and contradictory thoughts whirred through my head while I dawdled on the phone, further blotting out the description of the surgical process to come. One of the major questions, with a plaintive twist to it, was why me? Why did I happen across the one cat in a million that couldn't deliver a litter on her own? I was in the throes of finishing my fifth and final year of graduate school, having voluntarily submitted to penury in return for current wisdom and the promise of future earnings. Surely the animal gods that decide these matters could see that justice was better served by parachuting this needy kitty into a prosperous household, while sending a healthy one to broke little me.

Those eighth-grade mythology lessons about the Greeks shaking their fists in anger at the arbitrariness of the gods suddenly made sense.

Other thoughts flooded in too, some frankly more noble than others. A vague sense of annoyance wound its way into the mix, since this was positively inconvenient. So too did recurring feelings of victimization, seeing as this cat had sauntered into my life only four weeks earlier. True, we had bonded mightily in a short amount of time, but we weren't exactly BFFs—best friends forever. Not yet, anyway. Common courtesy and simple cat/person protocol require a longer courtship in advance of an avalanche of medical bills.

A slight tinge of anger and a whole lot of suspicion also entered my mind. Anger at the fact that I had been a lonely graduate student for years with no whiff of a friendly stray to share my life until a pregnant one arrives and cannot deliver by herself. Suspicion at the precise timing of it all—a cat walks into my life during the interregnum between conception and the birth of kittens. While I wasn't entirely sure this was an accurate assessment, it was a mighty reasonable hunch for a single guy with an empty wallet.

In Old West lingo, I was a-rubbing my chin thoughtfully with my fingers, doin' some mighty tall figurin' and realizin' that this here dadgum varmint cat had done sneaked herself into being taken care of, right under my watchful eyes.

This pushed an even more troubling thought into my head—one secretly shared by many males over the centuries. Was I even the appropriate surrogate father here, or was I the unwitting victim of female trickery? After all, this little vixen had quietly ensconced herself in my apartment without even disclosing the fact that she was expecting. Now she was going to cost me at least an entire month's income, probably without so much as a hint of appreciation or a trace of remorse. Meanwhile, I was stuck thinking through the kitty equivalent of child support payments, what with all of those little mouths to feed after the weaning ended and before I could place the little felines in homes, about eight weeks later. And then after all of this nurturing and care was meted out and finished, just what guarantee did I have that she was going to stick around with me for the long term? She might decide to walk right back out, having used me as one big sugar daddy, with a "thanks, schmuck" look on her face as she left.

The potentially troubling thought that these were not really my kittens was thankfully fleeting. Even the worn-out-by-graduate-school single male is able to keep enough of his wits about him to realize that the paternity of a litter of kittens is not the issue. One reason that God decided at the precise moment of creation that men on average should speak less than their counterparts was the grim realization that not all innermost male thoughts are worth airing.

"Uh-huh, okay, I understand" was my reply to the vet when he insisted again that the cat must be helped to deliver. My many years of college were finally paying off with mastery of the rhythm and range of the English language.

Alas, I must confess that some slightly untoward thoughts crept into this mix too. No question, my four-legged female friend was in some trouble here, but my two-legged female friend was an ardent cat lover. She owned two of those fancy-pants registered Persians— the kind of cat with the flat faces and the beautiful flowing manes, the show cats with the languorous eyes and the absolutely piss-poor attitude because every single stinking thing is handed to them on a silver platter.

Living with her two Persians in Minnesota at the time, this woman whom I frankly didn't know all that well was talking of visiting me for a short time en route to see her dad. Not clear to me was whether I was a desired destination or a convenient rest stop. But what did it really matter? How could she possibly resist my amorous intentions, I reasoned, once she heard this tale of woe? She would see nothing but unremitting heroism at paying for that which I could ill afford.

Hmm, a medical emergency that conveniently played into lasciviousness! Sweet deal. And talk about a winning hand. I could either tell my potential sweetie about the matter well in advance so that she had ample time to digest my masculine sensitivity, or I could hold all of the information back for dramatic effect upon her arrival, knowing that she would melt.

"Why yes," I rehearsed saying to her, "I did pay for a C-section for this precious little kitty, precisely because I knew it was the right thing to do, even though I really didn't have the money to do it while trying to pay my own way through graduate school." I said that over and over in my head to fix the sentiment in my mind. I likely practiced sounding impromptu.

The truth is, this unseemliness probably lingered just a bit longer than decency should have allowed. But for my still-living-in-South-

Dakota mother's sake, I am sticking to the story that this sexual connivance was pushed quickly from my mind.

But let's be fair, for not all of my thoughts were so calculating. What better place for a cattery, I reasoned, than the crummy apartment where I lived alone, and where the stick-it-to-the-transient-student landlady had already indicated to all of the tenants that we were pretty much destined to lose our security deposits?

"Oh, there are a lot of things to consider," the landlady had said, "and a good many extra expenses that you renters just don't see as we get the place ready for the next member of our apartment family." That was the company line she expected me to swallow when I gingerly inquired about the likelihood of receiving back my full month's security deposit.

Other reasonable thoughts included excitement and anticipation at having custody of some tiny kittens. Bemusement too, at the whole spectacle, sort of like actor Jack Lemmon at the end of the 1970 Neil Simon film, *The Out-of-Towners*, when New York can do nothing more to him and his wife than it has already done. Five years of living on the edge, I thought to myself, alone and without health or auto insurance, with no heat in one room where I lived and far too many cockroaches in another, and now working feverishly to mollify some well-intentioned professors who thought it best to have their graduate student keep pushing the frontiers of political science a little further with just a little more dissertation research.

At some point, the natural human reaction to cascading disaster is to laugh and mutter to oneself, "What the hell, bring it on. Yes, let's just have an unlikely surgery, a whole bunch of kittens, and expensive vet bills. Why not?"

But then an especially kind thought swept over me and prevailed. Here was one of the earth's small creatures, with nary a friend on this planet but me, fighting not only to live but to bestow new life. What could be more real, more touching? She would fight hard to cheat her early death, but she might not be able to overcome her physical limitations. Medical advances have taken much risk out of birthing processes, but even in modern times, there are no guarantees of a happy outcome.

The prospect of giving birth is terrifying and incomprehensible to men and bravely faced by females of all species throughout the ages. The drama necessarily evokes the tenderest thoughts within men; it certainly did in me. But we men feel so utterly helpless.

And sometimes we feel irritated with a world so indifferent to the pain and suffering of our loved ones. Perhaps my acute feeling for this cat was an artifact of my own narrow existence at the time (study, study, study, penny, penny, penny-pinch). But it somehow hurt to realize that this lone cat's painful ordeal was so unnoticed, and indeed so inconsequential, to the larger world. As I grew more silent and solemn over the phone about the perils she faced in the coming hours, as the fuller explanation of her situation continued, I wanted more than the vet and me to know and care about her troubles. But graduate students immersed in study are not much connected to the broader community, and they usually have few people to tell. Whatever the outcome, this event was therefore going to be like the funeral procession, when those involved want the world to note the significance of the day, but the disinterested observers can hardly wait for the hearse to pass so they can scurry along.

So my feelings were mixed and diffuse, but one thing was certain: if I agreed over the telephone to pay for this abdominal surgery for a stray cat taken in but a few weeks earlier, I would never live down the ribbing from my siblings, cat bashers of my acquaintance, or my college buddies. Some people occupied more than one of those categories.

My kind sister Mary loved me but generally disliked cats, not caring for their twirling and swirling underfoot. Close friends Steve and Terry were dog and fish guys, respectively, and Tim was a lukewarm pet guy, erring on the side of dogs. All of them had long ago pushed into the workplace and started families. What could be funnier to them than their old college buddy still in school after all these years, without more than a dime to his name, practically blubbering about his heroic efforts to save a cat?

And what would my parents think about their son when he confessed to destitution over a stray cat? They were both born on farms just outside of Irene, South Dakota, where almost the entire population of 400 people made their living by selling livestock and crops. One of my grandfathers had worked as a butcher, while the other had sold Pioneer brand seed corn to farmers and, for a brief time, had run something of a puppy mill on the side. Cat hospitalization? Not likely. Cat surgery? Out of the question.

So what were my parents likely to think? "Four years of financial sacrifice to provide that kid with a first-rate private liberal arts education at Augustana College," they might whisper to one another, "and we have raised a son with a very soft heart, and with a head to match."

* * *

By the time I finished talking with Dr. Biles on the telephone about the C-section, the expectant mother already had endured hours of unproductive labor, first at my apartment and then at the vet's office. Even the injection of the labor-inducing drug Pitocin had failed to produce the desired result.

Perhaps sensing silence, musing, and/or incomprehensible mumbling on my end of the line, the veterinarian briefly summed up the situation a final time, describing the actions taken and the absolute need to move ahead with abdominal surgery. Even before he finished, I marshaled an answer filled with male bravado.

"Go ahead and do that C-section," I said. "I'll figure out a way to pay for it."

He sounded relieved, maybe because he finally had a response from the apparently catatonic student on the other end. But it was also the case that Dr. Don Biles practiced with other vets at Westwood Veterinary in Norman, Oklahoma. He certainly would have performed the necessary operation out of a lifetime commitment to animals, but paying customers were always easier to explain to business partners. Decision concluded, we both hung up.

Seconds later, the phone rang again. Dr. Biles came straight to the point.

"When I open up your cat, do you want me to spay her too?" he asked. "It's just as easy as stitching her back together."

Now, South Dakota boys aren't called upon to make a whole passel of birthing decisions in their lifetimes, and it was beyond weird for me to end up in a free-flowing conversation about uterine removal. Before I could collect my thoughts, he added that it was all the same price, with or without the complimentary hysterectomy.

I have always considered my succinct reply an instinctive affirmation of the Humane Society's admonition to spay or neuter one's pet, but in truth this sounded like a straight-up bargain, an enticing two-for-one deal to a broke student.

"Yes, that would be fine," I blurted out. "Go ahead."

Only later did it occur to me that I had negotiated the fate of my cat's uterus over the telephone with a virtual stranger. I hoped she was comfortable with me making irreversible reproductive medical decisions for her.

* * *

The cat quite literally walked into my life. At the time, I was finishing up my last year of study toward a PhD in political science through the Department of Political Science and the Carl Albert Congressional Research and Studies Center at the University of Oklahoma. Named in honor of the former Speaker of the U.S. House of Representatives, the Carl Albert Center was filled with professors and graduate students devoted to the study of representative government. Director Ron Peters offered me a five-year fellowship at the Center, owing to a lengthy undergraduate thesis on Senate elections that was part of that fine liberal arts education my parents had paid for. Ron probably didn't think too much at the time about appearing in a cat book a few decades later.

Every day, I walked back from either Monnet Hall (home of the Carl Albert Center), or Dale Hall Tower (home of the political science department) to the student apartments known as Ashley Square. It was but a mile. The sun usually shone brightly in Oklahoma, so it was typically a nice walk. I was a former track and field runner in college, and I always liked to stretch my legs. And as a single male on a college campus with warm weather, what better than a leisurely walk to offer time to glance at the lovely coeds who attended OU. Eye candy, sightseeing—call it what you will, the traditional male sport of ogling had gained great popularity among campus men after *Playboy* magazine named an OU student with the exceedingly suspicious name of Candy Loving as its hallmark 25th Anniversary Playmate.

There was no easy place to park on campus and I couldn't afford a parking permit anyway. In fact, I carefully gauged each week how much I could afford to drive. So sauntering back to my apartment after a long day on campus of reading, writing, and thinking about a dissertation was all just part of the routine.

One sunny spring day, I returned to find a little white kitty perched on the landing, precisely halfway up the steps to my second-floor apartment.

She might have come from anywhere. Dozens of mostly impoverished students lived in Ashley Square, about six blocks southeast of one of the largest college football stadiums in North America. Our area was not the worst housing available—I had already lived there. But it wasn't exactly upscale either. Most of the inhabitants seemed to be international students, primarily from the Middle East, who were studying petroleum engineering at one of the great places in the world to do so. Many were stuck in the United States for an extended period because their families were affected by the vagaries of Iranian politics. At one point, demonstrations and fistfights had broken out at OU among the Iranian student supporters of the shah of Iran and those of Ayatollah Khomeini.

Guys who looked like FBI agents monitored the proceedings.

Resident Oklahomans clustered more in those gigantic fraternity and sorority houses over by Chautauqua Avenue, where they emerged smartly dressed to catch the university buses that arrived at their doors to take them to campus. Or they lived in dormitories, or the apartments west and southwest of the campus, down by the Lloyd Noble basketball arena. I had started out over there as well, but the small sum that I had borrowed initially to help pay for graduate school had long since been spent.

As I climbed the steps toward her, the little white kitty simply looked at me, without either affection or alarm. She swished her tail alongside her body as a preventive measure, probably assuming that anyone so large was not consistently agile. That mannerism would be repeated thousands of times in the years ahead, even after she concluded that I was watching out for her. In the cat's world, even a well-meaning oaf is still an oaf.

I knew relatively little about cats. My mother said that we had several mischievous souls who used to ride on my security blanket for sport as I toddled across the floor with it over my shoulder, but I have no memory of them or their antics. No cats in my life since, other than a brief interlude with Bob. He was owned by one of my college roommates at Augustana while we lived in the basement of a house a few blocks from campus. Bob spent most of his time climbing up the carpet we wrapped around a pole for his amusement. He studied fish in the aquarium. He partied with bacon bits while we drank beer. But we never really bonded. Three guys and a guy cat brought too much positioning about who was the alpha male.

One thing I had picked up from a high-school girlfriend was that cats appreciated a quiet approach and the opportunity to sniff a prospective friend. I had also learned those lessons through Bumper and Sticker, the white cats belonging to Judy, the campaign manager for South Dakota senator George McGovern's last reelection bid in the state. This sort of homage must appeal to a cat's sense of self-worth, I reasoned. Just a couple of steps short of the white kitty, I bent down very slowly and extended my fingers toward her nose.

She clearly appreciated the gesture, lifting her head ever so slightly to inhale the scent of her prospective friend. She sniffed briefly and then graciously bestowed upon me what I later called a "rubby"—a gentle nudging of my fingers with the side of her face.

Men are by nature a proud and sometimes vain lot. And I was certainly pleased by my clever little maneuver at this point, learning only much later in books about cats that they use scent glands on their face to mark their possessions. That should have been a clue that I was being played for a sugar daddy. But it was just as well that I thought she had provided me with a warm and uniquely personal greeting. The rubby prompted me to glance over my shoulder as I ascended the steps. I left the door slightly ajar, just in case.

She quickly bounded up the few remaining stairs. This is predictable behavior, summarized in this simple mathematical equation: Cat + Open Door = Oh My God, Anything Could Happen!

Several minutes passed as she canvassed the joint. She took stock of the furnishings, which were not much if the measure used was either quantity or quality. She stepped up on the living-room couch, a saggy plaid thing covered with a green blanket and made from the scratchy embedded fibers that cats just love to shred.

Go for it, missy, I thought.

I owned no furniture of my own. This dilapidated, sad-ass sofa was the property of the landlady who was probably going to keep my security deposit anyway, so a few claw marks blending into the tapestry seemed perfectly fitting.

The cat's exploration didn't take long. I had a combined living room/dining room (in other words, I had a table in the living room), a small bathroom and small kitchen, and a bedroom with a mattress on the floor. No headboard, no box spring. No dresser. No furnishings resembling the czar's winter palace in St. Petersburg. In retrospect, though, I did have one thing that the cat mentally noted while she was walking around—a low occupancy rate.

No population density problem here, she correctly surmised. *I count but a lone oaf.*

Little did I realize that she was furtively planning to share my limited personal space, and also to populate the place.

When, after stepping down from the couch, she headed in a straight line across the living room, I detected a limp. Her right rear leg dragged slightly behind her, flopping out a bit to the right, like it was twisted. But she did not seem to be in pain and was untroubled by her awkward gait. Apparently, animals are not susceptible to commercial messages about their imperfections and how to resolve them. They simply accept.

The lioness was unimpressed with the kingdom. After a short time, she nonchalantly walked out the open door and sat back down on the steps.

I was not well positioned to do anything generous for anyone at this point in my life. No tangible property or quality furnishings. Limited cash in a checking account, no savings account, and student loans looming on the horizon. Eyes hurting much of the time from too much reading, and fingers from too much typing. No regular woman in my life in Oklahoma—just a maybe girlfriend hundreds of miles away in Minnesota. No travel to distant places, no vacations to enjoy, no splurges on the weekends. Golf was too expensive. Diet consisted of cold food and boxed carbohydrates. Hair was starting to thin. God was in my thinking at the time, but mostly in terms of whether the afterlife that he would provide was going to be better than life here on earth, as the saints had promised. At times I rued the day that I ever learned Marx's observation that religion was simply an opiate of the masses.

I sometimes felt like if I stood on a random street corner in the southeast section of Norman, a strange dog might walk up right in the middle of the day and piss on my ankles.

The last few weeks had been especially rough. I had been yanked around quite a bit by a single member of an otherwise reasonable dissertation committee. He had put me in a surly mood. In the long run, he probably did me a service by pushing me so hard, but at this point in time I was mostly interested in finishing up and going on my way. If you've ever waited for what seems like forever in a Kmart checkout line, then faced the grim reality that your merchandise needs a price check, you know the heartache. Now imagine waiting in the line for five years before the price check happens.

If he were standing on a street corner in the middle of the day in the southeast section of Norman, with his back turned to me, I would have been tempted to target his ankles.

Against that backdrop of negativity, this wandering white kitty presented a pleasant diversion. And yes, I had in stock exactly what she wanted. Canned goods were the staples of my diet. And a good many of the cans were tuna because of my catlike fondness for oily fish and because cold sandwiches were an easy meal for the non-cooking bachelor. I usually rounded out the scrumptious tuna sandwich with some potato chips and a large chunk of lettuce topped with blue-cheese dressing, always along with iced tea, an Oklahoma favorite. The total cost of dinner was just a few bucks.

I popped open a can of Bumble Bee tuna and headed outside with a full plate. StarKist was too upscale.

She caught a whiff and headed straight for it. Now I understood why she hadn't stayed in my apartment for very long—she was actively searching for food. She wolfed down the entire contents of the can. As it disappeared, I scurried back for a saucer of milk, which she quickly disposed of as well. Little did I know she was eating for more than one.

Yet if she appreciated the hand extended for a rubby, the open door, the exploration, or the fine dining and drink, she didn't bother to express it. She began a long and laborious post-dinner grooming, restoring her white coat to its original luster. Tuna touching only her mouth evidently sullied her whole body, judging from all the production. The bath over, she limped down the apartment stairs and disappeared around the corner.

Gratitude is not a strong suit of cats.

2

The Swinging Door

I CHECKED THE APARTMENT steps several times and periodically looked out a window the rest of the evening, but the white kitty had disappeared. I figured that she had probably returned home for a second (and by comparison with tuna, unsatisfactory) meal and a prolonged nap. As darkness descended, I abandoned the watch. This seemed to be nothing other than a pleasant interlude on a single Oklahoma evening.

The next morning, I hoped she would be perched on the steps, providing another amusing diversion. But when the door was swung open, the white kitty was nowhere in sight. I dallied for a while, assembling and reconfirming materials in my backpack with great care, secretly thinking this might provide enough opportunity for her to wander back. Just to draw time out a little bit more, I sat down to slowly munch some cereal for breakfast. Before doing so, I cracked the door open again, just in case. But she didn't show.

It turns out that gratitude really is not a strong suit of cats.

The princess reappeared when I returned from school at about the same time as the day before. She was lounging at the very top of the apartment steps this time, and she was either deeply reflecting on her day or just possibly staring vacantly into space. It was my first clue that a perfect day in a cat's life is to recreate every single pleasant sensation of the day before in precisely the same order.

She was likely thinking through the exact sequence of events that resulted in the tuna treat the day before. You could almost hear the thoughts whirring: *Let's see now, was it that the oaf appears from no-where, followed by a rubby and tuna? Or was it the oaf, apartment explo-ration, and then food? Or did I just find the food sitting on the floor of the apartment of the dim-witted oaf? Or did the oaf hand-deliver the plate outside? No, maybe that was the milk. Damn, one day does not establish a consistent routine.*

So we again met with a rubby, but this time she waltzed in the open door right on my heels. We were still following the process-es, but apparently dispensing with the formalities. Tuna was surely on her mind, but without any knowledge of where the bounty was stashed, she followed me into the sort-of-a-kitchen only after the lid popped and the scent trickled out across the room. Once again, my new friend ate most heartily, lolling her tongue around for a long time, as if to live and relive the consummate culinary experience. I once did the same thing in a Florida restaurant after my dad bought me king crab legs.

Perhaps realizing the error of her ways on the previous day, when she bathed on a hard concrete landing, this time she plunked down on the comfort of my carpeted floor. Little did I realize that this event marked the beginning of what I would come to call the Era of the White Fur, a definable time in my life when every single one of my worldly possessions was coated in her white cat hair.

Following the ritualistic cleanup, she wandered in and out of my open door the rest of the evening. She liked that. It allowed her to balance her contradictory desires for safety and adventure. Closed doors offended her.

At bedtime that evening, I faced a quandary. The open-door policy was fine during daylight hours, but it had to be suspended at night for my own safety. Nothing against my neighbors, but this wasn't exactly a gated and patrolled community. Hotheads were rumored to be out there, dogs and lunatic graduate students looking to piss on people's ankles. My new friend could be on only one side of the door, and for all that I knew, she already had a nice home. She may have wolfed down the tuna simply because no self-respecting cat would pass it up. I had no idea if she was truly hungry, though she seemed it.

Over her vocal protest, I scooped her up in my arms and set her just outside the door, figuring she would head home. She eventually wandered off, but only after instilling massive guilt. Whenever I quietly tiptoed over to the door to peek at her through the peephole, to see if she had departed, she flipped her head around and looked straight back at the door.

Not even tiptoeing oafs can sneak up on cats.

As I lay down in bed that night, I recalled the brief but pleasant sensation of holding her in my arms for the first time. It seemed so natural. It felt like love at first sight.

The same pattern repeated itself for several more days. She would be waiting right there on the steps when I returned from campus, devour a meal, wander in and out of the open apartment door for the evening, and then be scooped up and placed outside for the night. With each successive evening, I found it more heartrending to place her on the other side of the door, and she more vehemently protested her removal. Even so, she was always gone in the morning—until one day later in the week. By that time, I was acting like a little kid at Christmas, but trying to sneak a peek outside for a cat instead of under the tree for presents. The resilience of youth allowed me to take time to swing open the apartment door first thing in the morning, even before the bathroom door.

Our eyes met on that special morning when she was there, standing right outside the door. At that moment, at that very instant, both of us experienced the melding of two lonely souls for all eternity.

At least that's how it would have worked in an ideal world. The grim truth is that she dished out an icy stare and a severe tongue-lashing of successive meows.

Come on, dumbass, her yowl seemed to say, *figure this out.* As she strolled past me into the apartment, she seemed to add, *By the way, what are we having for breakfast?*

In my defense, I was not as slow-witted as the cat might have believed. I had secured packets of Tender Vittles a day or two earlier, in part because she had been oversampling my personal stash of not-so-expensive-except-to-me tuna. Even talking up mercury poisoning had not deterred her. If this relationship was going to survive and thrive, we had to eat within our means.

Frankly, the combination of things was starting to unnerve me— the icy stare, the constant hunger, my growing doubts about whether she had a proper home, the mild limp, and my guilt over sleeping inside each night while she faced unknown perils outside.

Ultimately, what other choice did I have?

I locked the cat *inside* the apartment. I descended the stairs and stepped onto the same narrow sidewalk that had led me to meet up with her on my apartment steps. I hopped into my 1974 AMC Gremlin, later identified by car enthusiasts as one of the ten worst cars ever built. It was purchased on the used-car lot of Fait Chevrolet in Canton, South Dakota, with money earned from summers working in the steel factory for my dad. Dad worked me like a dog those summers, partly to keep me out of bars at night but also to provide a reminder of the need to get the good liberal arts education that life never gave him a chance to pursue.

My AMC Gremlin was unique. It had no extras like cruise control or air-conditioning, the absence of which was excruciating during Oklahoma summers. And it was painted purple, a two-door hatchback. But this graduate-student limousine that I'd owned for seven years had a special feature, one that raised its price at Fait Chevrolet by $150. It had an authentic Levi's denim interior. Yes, it did. You sat your blue-jean-covered butt right on blue-jean seats. Two red stickers affixed to either side of the car above the front wheels proudly proclaimed "Levi's" to the whole world. In retrospect, it was fitting that the AMC Gremlin was launched with the public on April Fool's Day in 1970.

I backed out of the parking lot of Ashley Square and took a right toward the city park. Next was a right on Lindsey Street, past the university duck pond. The street continued on toward the railroad tracks. Just to drive home my point about the loveliness of the neighborhood, a drunk guy was run over by a train on those tracks while I lived there, only a long stone's throw from my apartment. No more ogling OU girls for him. I stayed on Lindsey until I reached the shopping mall with the Safeway store for those of us living on this side of town. There was usually plenty of parking. Few other Norman residents made their way over to shop at this particular Safeway location.

"Let's see," I whispered to myself in the aisle of Safeway, as is typical of the person who lives alone. "We need some food, a litter box, a scooper, and a couple of inexpensive cat toys to make this official."

I loaded them up in the car, bounced back across the tracks, past the duck pond a second time, and turned into Ashley Square. Left off so far in the telling of this tale is that my apartment lacked much of a birds-eye view; in fact, it faced squarely into the back of a concrete building. The view each morning when I headed out the door was the back of that building. No wonder the cat always had a blank look on her face when she sat on the steps and surveyed the area. No birds-eye view and no rodents scampering about the base of the concrete wall.

* * *

The white princess was thoroughly confused by my trip to the store. She complained loudly upon my return at being locked inside the apartment for the first time. I tried hard to assuage and redirect her with a display of cat food and toys, but the toys were of the cheap ball variety, and she later proved to be a confirmed string kitty. Nothing had the desired salutary effect until the closet was rearranged to accommodate the litter box. All the explanation she needed was right there; I laugh to myself even now, recalling how the light clicked on in her head. At bedtime on that beautiful evening in Norman, as she softly crawled right on top of my chest, two inches from my nose, my cares and worries seemed to vanish like darkness at the dawn of a new day.

I can never properly express in words the close bond that she and I forged that night. Attempts to do so, even with those I love, have always fallen short. Though it sounds trite, perhaps genuine companionship and love is only felt, not explained. My spiritual and wise mother would later observe that the little white kitty was sent by none other than a guardian angel to salve my spirit at a lonely and difficult time in my life.

The white kitty purred incessantly and kneaded the comforter endlessly as I gently stroked and softly spoke to her. I stayed awake for a very long time, rubbing her head and ears and scratching her chin. She leaned into it all, stretching her neck and shifting her head around to ensure that every sweet spot was scratched. "Hey, sweetie," I murmured to her, "it's so good to have you here." She lapped up every moment of our first truly prolonged physical contact. Two lonely and needy souls had found one another, bringing us both peace and joy.

Later in life, when I finally had enough discretionary money to purchase books about cats and their behaviors, I learned that the practice of kneading simulates the kitten's attempts to get milk from its mother. Kneading of humans by adult cats probably indicates a regressed subservience to a mother figure.

Oh, the delicious irony. Male, twenty-seven years old, living completely alone, and a little white kitty had miraculously turned me into a single mother.

3

Two New Mothers

THE WHITE KITTY HAD met up with Dr. Biles one time prior to her abdominal surgery. I took her in for the "once over" after she conclusively moved in with me. Her bum leg in particular needed a look. She vigorously protested my lack of consultation about automobile travel, seeing few virtues in it. Perhaps she was embarrassed about being seen around town in a purple Gremlin, or maybe she was just plain hot, since I didn't have air-conditioning. The only thing she relished about my car was the denim Levi's seats; they were one ready-made cat scratching post, conveniently located throughout the car.

"Hey, as long as I'm bored and don't know where we're going," she seemed to say, "let me just sharpen up these claws." An unfortunate but understandable attitude, given the free reign she had back at our apartment with the keep-my-deposit landlady's scuffed-up furniture.

"Honey, please don't scratch up my car seats," I would plead while driving, with her just out of reach. "We have to keep this car looking good. We can't afford a new one."

All that persuasion returned a blank stare.

Constant reassurance from me as we sped about that everything would be okay also fell on deaf ears. Should I have been surprised? Cats hear more selectively than any of God's other creatures. Words hitting their ears are effortlessly and immediately jettisoned, or if retained, considered purely advisory, not binding.

The white kitty was neither enthralled nor alarmed at being at the veterinarian's office. Likely she had never been to a vet before, and cats never mind the first visit. It's all subsequent visits that are out of the question. The waiting room, or holding pen, as we might have thought of it in South Dakota, was mercifully quiet, and my cat knew not what evils lurk in such places. The pattern of my precious fluff ball turning into a sinister beast at the vet was still some time off. While this is difficult to admit, my little white angel had a very dark side when it came to vet visits. In fact, later in life she once tried—through vicious slashing—to even the score for all kitties of the world vis-à-vis their veterinarian oppressors.

Dr. Biles was very adept. He obviously loved kitties and knew how to handle them. He patiently and diligently examined her respirations, heart rate, and teeth; he diagnosed a case of ear mites (the plague of many outdoor kitties); and he offered a prescription remedy costing almost nothing. Whew. He even took her body temperature without much incident. That particular procedure greatly offends a cat's sense of decorum.

The white kitty did shoot him a bit of an "uh, excuse me?" look.

After that was done, Dr. Biles looked me squarely in the eye and drily observed, "Your cat will be having kittens soon."

Huh? What? I was caught off-guard, stunned. I was only capable of stammering the universal male response to an announced pregnancy: "Are you sure?"

CHAPTER THREE

Dr. Biles paused for a moment. As an older veterinarian, he had probably seen more than a few thousand pregnant kitties in his lifetime, and he was weighing the appropriate response to the dimwitted questioner. What he could have replied was very different from what he graciously offered, which was a wink, a nod, and a "Yes, I'm pretty sure."

What news. The princess was more than the solitary little white kitty that I had gently caressed and softly addressed our first night together. She was a walking family unit with her own set of issues and timetables. Kneading me so diligently was more than a sign that I was her mother—it was a warning that I was about to become a grandmother.

Dr. Biles gently felt her abdomen and speculated that as many as four kittens were on the way. The extra mouths to feed were a concern, but that was not much on my mind at this point, since their momma would take care of it initially. Nor was I worried about the kittens trashing my apartment, since I really owned nothing of value. But I was a little nervous at the prospect of becoming a father, or a mother, or a grandmother, or whatever it was that I was becoming. My parents came from the farm, but I was born and raised in Sioux Falls, a lifelong city kid with much less exposure to the birthing process than my rural cousins. I was but waiting-room material.

I asked the typical man questions: "How long before she delivers? How will I know when it all starts? What will I need to do? Will you be around if we need help?"

She would deliver in a few weeks, Dr. Biles informed me. He didn't say it this way, but even a stupid blooming idiot would know when the birthing process was starting. My only responsibility would be to provide a secluded, comfortable place.

"She will do the rest," he assured me.

I let out an audible sigh of relief.

While total seclusion was illusory in a one-bedroom apartment, she would have a safe and quiet place.

Dr. Biles finally turned to the issue of her limp. He speculated that a dog had bitten the kitty's leg, severely twisting it. The weight of the kittens exacerbated the problem, he said, but improvement would come swiftly after she delivered. Nothing had to be done. It looked worse to us than it felt to her, he said.

This welcome news meant less pain for the cat and less cost to the graduate student.

As I headed out the door with the expectant mother, Dr. Biles curiously asked, "How did you come up with that name—Frodo?" A reasonable question, and one that I answered many times before Hollywood made the name famous by turning some long-published novels into blockbuster adventure movies.

"Frodo is the main character in the J. R. R. Tolkien books about hobbits," I replied, "and a bit of a wayward soul, but a hero." Ah, the splendid smugness of that moment, made possible by inside knowledge of great literature, owing to that high-quality liberal arts education.

Dr. Biles paused as he first tried to translate that sentence, then just shrugged his shoulders. The vet tech working his way through OU at the time overheard the conversation as I spilled back into the waiting area, and he grinned broadly. I knew immediately that he grasped the reference. And so before he even said a word, I explained further to him: "I know it's unusual, but she might be the only cat that I'll ever have, and I always wanted a Frodo. Plus, she has a hobbit's furry feet." He smiled and nodded knowingly. He clearly understood why the expectant mother bore the name of a fictional male character.

* * *

The Great Birthing Event began as I was bumming around the apartment, suffering from a stint of dissertation writer's block. The scholarly problem was how best to reframe my literature review to place my work on religious interest groups more in the context of existing research on legislative agenda setting; the real obstacles to progress were preoccupation with my newfound friend and too much daydreaming about better days ahead. John Lennon's lyrics "you may say I'm a dreamer" had become my unofficial anthem.

I noticed Frodo lying atop the comforter on my bed, looking, well, a bit quizzical. Mere seconds later, her water broke. I quickly grabbed a towel and tucked it underneath as she lay there, hoping to save my prized blue-and-white checked comforter purchased at the local Target store from any further birthing activity. I didn't exactly have a linen closet full of replacement bedding.

Frodo promptly moved over one foot to be off it. Sensing a losing proposition, I went over by the bedroom closet to remind her of the specially prepared kitty delivery cardboard box with the high walls and soft towel, currently unoccupied. But from a cat's perspective, this was simply an ill-timed game of human show-and-tell. She completely ignored my plea. This small setback was subsequently revised in my mind to reflect my unremitting heroism for providing Frodo a much-needed focal point during labor. Men do help in that way, after all.

The delivery drama continued. I perceptively figured out that it wouldn't take a cat very long to give birth, given nature's inherent proclivities to protect species from harm. Advanced biology class at Washington High School, more biology at Augustana College, and a better-than-*Reader's Digest* understanding of Darwin in the Galapagos Islands were blending together exquisitely in my head at this critical moment to yield great medical insights. The birth of kittens must happen almost right away, I astutely reasoned. And this must be virtually automatic, given the many cats in the world. Smiling at my own wisdom, I thought to myself, *Hey, big guy, your firm grasp of the life sciences is paying dividends today.*

Of course, I didn't really know anything about cat birthing processes other than the primer given to me by the vet at our single visit.

In thinking about the birthing process that morning, I realized that Frodo was a week or so past the projected delivery date announced by Dr. Biles. That should have been a clue that something was amiss, but I truly didn't think much about it. My one shred of obstetrical knowledge was that women often went past their delivery dates, and it usually worked out fine—as if that insight was a comparable medical fact.

By early evening, though, I became concerned about the lack of progress. I called the vet's office to seek guidance. One of the vets in the practice, on call for the evening, telephoned back. He listened carefully but counseled patience for this first-time mother, emphasizing that cats only rarely have birthing problems. Greatly relieved, I hung up and spent most of the evening quietly petting Frodo. She seemed content enough, but somewhat more insistent than usual that I stay nearby.

I crawled into the available side of the bed later that night, thinking it was damn odd for a young guy to be sharing his bed with a birthing cat, but figuring that where she went in the wee hours to finish this whole thing was outside my control. *Take that, you keep-my-deposit landlady*, I snidely thought to myself. *Going to use up my deposit and your profit at the same time by cleaning the carpet? Ha, ha, ha.*

The fact that Frodo hadn't delivered was starting to bother me. Though it was unwarranted, I grew increasingly perturbed at the vet on call, retrospectively reasoning that he could have taken a little more time away from his evening engagement to talk me through

this situation. But I let it go. Sifting through my arsenal of biologi-
cal knowledge some more, I concluded that it only made sense that
Frodo would deliver during the night. Nature logically pushes cats in
the direction of nocturnal birth for their own safety, I reasoned, again
without a shred of knowledge about the subject. Besides, what did I
really know about labor and delivery timetables for new cat mothers?
Perhaps Great Birthing Events always took this long.

I was teaching American Government to 120 students early the
next morning in Dale Hall on the OU campus, so I decided I would
just wake up early to check on her. I fully expected to arise to the
meow of tiny kittens in the box in the closet, if they could meow right
away. I didn't really know that either.

* * *

Instead, I awoke to a very distressed cat. She was insistent that we stay
close, a quiet plea for help after too many hours of labor. I tried comforting her, but I also felt obliged to head to the university to teach
my class. A superb teaching record was critical to finding a suitable
job after graduate school, and student evaluations of teaching were
a principal piece of information sought by hiring institutions. Four
years at Augustana College, followed by five years of graduate study
at the University of Oklahoma—this was no time to give the heave-
ho to my responsibilities in the classroom. Teaching the class meant
only one more hour away from Frodo after so many in labor, so I felt
it was the sensible, if rather disconcerting, thing to do.

Besides, there was no easy way to cancel class. Graduate students
were assigned the much-loathed 8:00 a.m. time slot—the very same
time the departmental office opened in nearby Dale Hall Tower
and the university came alive. Faculty usually picked afternoon or
evening classes, leaving graduate students to fill out the other hours.
Recorded phone messages were not an option then, and email was

not yet available. There was no way to cancel an 8:00 a.m. class other than to call precisely at 8:00 a.m., hoping that a departmental secretary arrived at work on time and was ready to traipse over from Dale Hall Tower to the Dale Hall classroom building to announce, "Class dismissed."

Sickness sometimes required that call, but staying away voluntarily really wasn't an option. Especially not for a South Dakota kid ingrained with a strong work ethic at the hand of his father at the steel factory over the course of several summers.

It still bothers me that in being so conscientious, I prolonged her suffering. But at least I did one right thing—I decided to use up some of my monthly gasoline allocation by driving to work that day, so it was possible to return speedily to Ashley Square after class was over.

I lectured to the American Government class, but truthfully I have no recollection of the subject. My head was elsewhere, and so was my heart. Teaching class on that day mostly consisted of showing up and going through the motions. In fact, I cut class short, stammering at the end that I had to shoot back to my apartment to see if my kitty cat that was having so much trouble delivering her kittens had finished the job.

This was the first my students had heard of any of this. It must have struck them as a rather odd transition from whatever political topic we were discussing that day. "Did I hear him right?" they must have asked one another. "Did he say that he was going to a cat birthing?"

Racing out of class, I walked swiftly to the car, hopped into the Gremlin, sped down Lindsey Street, turned right onto George Street, pulled into the Ashley Square parking lot, and quickly trotted toward the door. Rather odd and frenetic behavior, in the wake of doing nothing for hours on end. Frodo noted my arrival, picking her head up when I entered the bedroom, but she was visibly exhausted. The customary gleam in her eyes that came with having a home and feeling loved had given way to a dull gloss. Her body language and her plaintive voice cried out for help.

As fast as my fingers could dial a white rotary phone, with its seemingly interminable spins, I connected with the vet's office. "Hi, this is Matt Moen," I started out. "You know, the guy with the cat that started giving birth yesterday, but now she hasn't finished the job and I'm really worried about her. She doesn't look well. Her name is Frodo."

The words coming back to me from the other end of the line were kind and calm, but some urgency in the voice was palpable. "Bring her in right now," the vet's office told me.

I felt horrible on the short drive across town. My desperate little friend was utterly bewildered and enfeebled. She hated to go in the car, especially at a time when she felt so vulnerable. Then to arrive at the worst of all places, filled with potentially frightening dog smells to a birthing cat mother. Once I arrived, a vet tech grabbed Frodo out of my arms and headed off into a back room, pausing momentarily to shout back that they would call me. Embarrassed by my ineptitude leading to this ignominious moment, and also just a wee bit pissed at the injustice of this sorry sequence of events, I slunk home to wait by the telephone.

The short drive to the vet's office was a painfully long drive back to my apartment.

Time passed excruciatingly slow. I had met Frodo only weeks before, but she had already moved into the center of my life. We had shared some incredibly tender and loving moments at a time in my life when these were lacking. *Had I now unwittingly allowed her to die?* I wondered. Why had I failed to insist on greater care or more answers when I had called the vet the night before? How was it possible to have turned my back on her for even a brief time on this day, placing a government lecture ahead of a life? Dejected, I sat down on my lumpy sofa with cat claw marks and fought back tears. I mumbled a quiet prayer for her health and well-being, not entirely convinced that this would do any good, but hoping that the residual Lutheranism challenged by my secular studies of politics still had enough clout to somehow pull this thing through with a happy ending.

The first call came in early afternoon. I jumped to answer the phone. Having failed to induce her successfully with Pitocin to deliver the kittens, Dr. Biles would have to perform a cesarean section. The second call about the complimentary hysterectomy came only seconds later. Waiting resumed.

Gradually, though, the sadness was replaced with the agitation of the expectant father. *Everything must be going okay, since they took time to induce her before skipping to surgery,* I reasoned. Cesarean sections usually worked out pretty well for women, whatever was involved in the procedure. This would work out too.

Finally, a call came from the receptionist, who said it was time to return to the office. The purple Gremlin barreled down the streets of Norman as if it were one of the ten zippiest automobiles ever built, not one of the ten worst. "Family medical emergency" was the excuse on the tip of my tongue, should I be stopped by a cop.

Ushered into an exam room, I waited impatiently for Dr. Biles. The receptionist had given up nothing on the phone, and the staff said nothing about the condition of Frodo or her kittens when I was brought into the exam room. I spent some brief but tense moments looking at the posters on the walls about keeping one's pets healthy. *Failed the big preventative keep-your-pet-healthy test, you big chump,* I thought to myself. Perhaps it was divine retribution that these posters now loomed larger than life.

Tension mounted. This didn't feel right; the office staff should have piped up with an "everything's okay" sort of greeting when I walked into the office. They hadn't.

Dr. Biles entered the room and cut to the chase.

"Frodo is fine," he said, "and she appears to be a good mother."

Relief rolled over me like a tidal wave. I asked about the number of kittens, mentally calculating the number of Tender Vittles packets that would be required to feed the entourage at some point. Dr. Biles replied quietly, with genuine sadness in his voice.

"Frodo was carrying four kittens," he said. "Two of them were dead in her uterus and even slightly necrotic, which is why she was having so much difficulty delivering."

A third kitten was born alive, he said, but it lived for only a few minutes. Injection of some drug to keep it alive failed. In retrospect, I've always thought that particular kitten was an especially tragic loss because Dr. Biles said the kitten was a white female—the closest thing to Frodo's clone.

The fourth kitten, however, had survived this cruel Darwinian selection process. He sported a mostly gray coat, while sharing his mother's white fur on his feet, nose, and chest. At first glance, he appeared to be your typical cat. As you will learn, he was not.

Having conveyed all of the necessary medical information, Dr. Biles disappeared for a brief moment. He reemerged with a very proud and contented momma cat, curled around her new son in a small box emptied of vet supplies. The two of them fit perfectly.

Frodo's ordeal was over. Like me, she too was a mother.

4

Switched at Birth

CHOOSING TO USE UP another of my monthly
gasoline allotments was one way of living it up in the aftermath
of Frodo's return home, so two days later I drove triumphantly to
Dale Hall for my American Government class. Luckily, the Gremlin managed more than twenty miles per gallon. And this was
the state of Oklahoma, where stripper oil wells had collectively
produced copious amounts of oil for decades, keeping down the
price of gas. Living it up with some extra driving was a smaller
financial sacrifice than in most parts of the country, so this was
the perfect way to splurge.

Haggard and emotionally wrung out, I shuffled into the classroom at about 7:57 a.m., just minutes before class was to start.

Because I didn't follow my usual routine and engage the students
right away upon walking into the room, they quietly sized up my face,
body language, and mood, rather than ask. I had left them hanging,
with sad news of a cat in distress. In fact, I had dashed out of class
with the sudden desire to be a chivalrous knight rescuing a damsel

in distress, after sitting around for hours like a peasant in a castle siege. I sensed immediately that the students wanted to know the outcome, but most of them being kids from Oklahoma, they were too polite to push the point, willing to patiently wait until I was settled and ready to make the announcement. They were also being graded at the semester's end, of course, so no one was exactly anxious to stick their neck out by tendering the implicit question, "So did your cat die, Mr. Moen?"

People with good news sometimes keep it to themselves a little longer than they should. This is partly selfish, but mostly a temporary form of control, or a matter of personal privilege. Those of us raised in the Midwest do this with little things because slightly holding back is a time-honored antidote to the immediate boasting in other parts of the country; Garrison Keillor's characters in Lake Wobegon are so darn believable to Midwesterners precisely because they exhibit characteristic understatement.

I waited until about 8:02 a.m. before really looking up from my notes to engage and address the quizzical faces of the 100 or so students who showed up for the lecture. Turnout of 100 percent of the class would have been better for an instructor now bursting at the seams to tell the primarily happy ending to a story left in progress, but this wasn't too bad for the first slot on a Wednesday morning. My shuffling around of my lecture notes on the podium to bide time now having run its course, the moment had arrived to bring the students up to speed.

"When we left off the other day," I solemnly started, "you may recall that I had to rush out of here because my cat was struggling to deliver kittens. Sorry about that."

Their faces signaled back to me, "Yeah, yeah, we remember. Get on with it."

"Well," I began, more slowly than was really fair, "I'm happy to report to you that things went well. My cat Frodo is back home all safe and sound, and she appears to be a good mother. We have one kitten."

Dr. Biles's observation about Frodo being a good mother had stuck in my head, and it was just now repeated verbatim to the students. That sort of verbal plagiarism seemed like a no-no in my business, but I felt lucky to have a second good mom in my life.

College students being a nice lot—right at that perfect age where they have separated from their parents but still can be kids at heart—they spontaneously clapped and cheered, and a few even whistled their approval. Some of the students might have been slightly sarcastic in their exuberance, but I was on cloud nine and chose to interpret all of the noise in a completely positive way. A full minute passed before I was able to tuck away my smile.

Then I backed up and started telling them in excruciating detail how Frodo and one kitten survived, while its three siblings died, including one whose life had hung in the balance. Glossed over was my thought that the third kitten might have lived if the vet had been brought into the picture sooner, but, hey, not all details can make their way into such a story, especially in a tight fifty-minute lecture block. Besides, Dr. Biles had listened to my confession like a good Catholic priest and absolved me of any wrongdoing. And there was no need to admit forgiven sins. Not even Dante's *Inferno* meted out punishments to the absolved.

The students truly enjoyed the full story told by the earnest graduate student learning to teach by experimenting on them, although Oklahoma taxpayers probably didn't get their full money's worth on that particular day. Tuition-paying parents might have liked to grab a partial refund, or see an area dog target my ankles.

Individual students asked about Frodo for the rest of the semester, prefacing their questions about course material or assignments with a friendly "So, how's Frodo?" Others pigeonholed me and regaled me with stories about their own pets. Those were sweet, although secretly I thought they paled in comparison. Still, it was darn nice that college kids took an interest in this aspect of my life. Not too many people pondered my doleful existence.

Frodo's principal contribution to my life was the sheer joy she brought during some of my darkest months; a secondary contribution was her accidental boosting of my budding career. Her improbable delivery caught the imagination of my students. Accustomed to omnipotent professors, the students were amused by a graduate student intertwining lectures on politics with cat tales. Many of them provided highly favorable course evaluations at the end of the semester, increasing my marketability to higher-education institutions.

Of course, a few students were not thrilled by my rhetorical beeline to the feline. In response to a standard open-ended question about what the instructor could do to improve his or her teaching, one student wrote on the form, and I do quote, "tell fewer kitty stories."

Anonymous musings from some dog-loving fiend, I thought to myself.

An unfortunate consequence of good course evaluations was feeling even guiltier for having taken a birthing Frodo to the veterinarian *after* class. Cat boosted career. Career placed before cat. At least the lesson was not lost on me. Gratitude is much stronger in humans.

Of course, there's also a distinct possibility that Frodo acted out of calculated self-interest when she caused such a stir. In this scenario, she mutters to herself, "The big oaf is sweet, but he is without a full-time job and a spacious apartment. He owns crappy furnishings.

He is clearly struggling. A better life for me means making something more out of him, which is no easy task. Might require some hubbub and heroics on my end."

Desperate times do call for desperate measures, I suppose.

* * *

Frodo had no idea how her story captured the hearts of others. I can't recall specific details of the long-distance telephone conversations that immediately followed the C-section, but it's easy to convey their essence. My folks were genuinely pleased and greatly humored by the outcome of the birthing episode, and they were increasingly appreciative of Frodo's presence in my life. They soon met her on their own turf.

My cat-loving woman friend in Minnesota—the one who owned the two registered Persians—was elated. Although I had flirted with the idea of holding all of this information back until some future visit, there was no way I could do that. However, there was a catch in relaying the actual events. In my excitement to tell the story—the whole story, so that she could fully and completely digest my male sensitivity—I stumbled badly. Included was a brief explanation of how the short delay in getting Frodo to the vet during the waning hours of her labor didn't matter after all.

This was not a well-formulated strategy. The fear of abandonment during labor and delivery has to be any woman's deep-seated nightmare. Glibly suggesting to a woman of childbearing age that some extra labor did not really matter was none too bright.

Okay, it bordered on downright stupid.

Stunningly, stunningly stupid.

Quickly sensing a problem, I began muddling the precise sequence of events as I told and retold the story to her. Unfortunately, glossing over the part about the extra labor was a particular problem because my female friend worked as a registered nurse in the obstetrical wing of Mercy Hospital in suburban Minneapolis.

I was totally screwed.

I backpedaled. I kept fudging. The story became more and more convoluted, told way out of sequence. Sensing I was getting pinned down, I started playing up an entirely different angle—the bewildered bachelor unselfishly spending his few precious pennies to save a cat's life. Once I sensed this was working, I mercilessly pressed it. Unknowingly, Frodo was helping to draw another female into my life.

* * *

I called him Windsor initially, thinking it a distinguished name for the surviving and sole son of my beautiful white princess; it smacked of the British royal family. But he ignored it. Maybe deep down he knew that he was a total mutt living in a cheesy joint.

I experimented with several names after that, eventually settling on Brandy. It seemed to please him the most. Later on, I read that cats typically prefer names ending in *e* or *y* sounds. That discovery confirmed the wisdom of his name, but it caused consternation when I thought about my beloved Frodo. To ease my troubled conscience, I began to use the nickname Frody interchangeably with her proper name.

Brandy's name was appropriate because it lent itself to screeching, as in "Brandyyy!" His irregular entrance into the world convinced him that life had to be lived to the fullest. He was an unwitting disciple of founding father Ben Franklin: "Do not squander time, for that's the stuff life is made of."

Brandy never squandered time in his early days. He shredded, climbed, or tipped over every one of my household possessions at one time or another. Like a fit Olympic decathlete, he rested only between events.

His destructive nature was probably influenced by many factors. His very survival in the womb proved that he was the most rough-and-tumble kitten of the litter. His utter lack of playmates pushed him to seek out diversions and ensured him an endless supply of energy. No effort of his was wasted beating up on his brothers or sisters. The lack of any quality household possessions likely prevented me from exercising the requisite discipline, apart from the occasional clap of my hands to accompany a sharply pitched, uh, catcall. Even before the theme was popularized by substandard made-for-television movies on the Lifetime network, I started thinking that somehow Brandy had been switched at birth with Frodo's real kitten. What other explanation existed? How could an angel give birth to a demon?

Brandy may have also sensed that he was a third wheel, a message driven home by Frodo on the first night all three of us were together. I brought the two kitties home in the small box supplied by the vet, and they lay together for quite a long time. Before the evening ended, though, Frodo stepped out of the box in search of a few bites, companionship, and like all new mothers, a bit of personal space. The box provided by the vet seemed to her more of a mobile unit than a suitable home, so I offered her as a substitute the somewhat larger box with the old towel that was supposed to have been used for the birthing process. I ever so gently lifted the blind and helpless Brandy into that bigger box. Frodo monitored this transfer with incredible interest, but without alarm. The box was still sitting in the bedroom closet.

At bedtime, I was blessed with an unmistakable sign of Frodo's love. And Brandy faced the grim reality that his mom's loyalties were divided, at best. Since that first night we spent together, Frodo and I had established a set routine. After I crawled into bed, she moved right on top of my chest, purring incessantly and gently kneading me as I struggled to drop off to sleep. The routine was so pleasant that Frodo saw no reason to suspend it.

When I crawled under the covers that night, she promptly hopped out of the box where she was nestling Brandy, and strolled over to take her customary place on my chest. Brandy's tiny, plaintive cry reverberated through the quiet bedroom. I frankly didn't know kittens could sound off so soon after being born. Frodo stood straight up with ears held high, looked at the box and back at me, and then headed off to reassure her son. She did this over and over again with brief interludes throughout the night—no small feat for a gal that had just gone through a long labor and surgery. A couple of times, I arose from the bed and sleepily ambled over to the box, patting it and gently encouraging Frodo to step inside. She was enthused when I did so, but she kept following me back to the bed each time I thought she was happily situated. Frodo's affection for me was genuine. And I learned later in those cat books I purchased that new cat mothers often seek out extra reassurance.

Although I was certainly flattered by Frodo's intense loyalty, I also felt some sadness for Brandy. In retrospect, Frodo probably just needed space or some established routine after her harrowing experience.

In any event, the three of us had a restless first night. Brandy demanded his mother's presence when he was cognizant of her absence. Frodo tried to split her time between the two fellas in her life. I tried convincing Frodo to stay in the box with Brandy, keeping myself awake in the process.

Someone could have warned me that motherhood was so tiring.

The next night, I placed the box next to my bed, right up by my head. Since the bed was but a mattress on the floor, Frodo could move effortlessly back and forth between the two of us. To keep a solitary Brandy warm in an occasionally chilly apartment, I put an old heating pad beneath the towel in the box.

Frodo wholeheartedly approved. She could lie on my chest and look down into the box at Brandy, comforted by the fact that he was in sight. She also loved the heated box, perhaps a little bit more than she reveled in my company, truth be told. Frodo spent much of the next couple of weeks in that toasty cardboard box, coming out only when it was too hot to stay in. This arrangement also worked for me. I managed some sleep and yet kept her close at a time when another male was so important in her life.

Frodo seemed happy. She grew a little stronger each day, and she slowly regained her good looks as the fur grew over her tummy incision. Her eyes sparkled. "And how is my beautiful white princess today?" I would ask rhetorically, one of a thousand variations on a theme.

* * *

Frodo's tranquility ended with Brandy's mobility. All of the will and determination he exhibited in a necrotic womb carried over in attempts to clamber out of his box. Perhaps he was seeking out other siblings, or perhaps he was just plain bored with the four brown walls; either way, he began scaling the ramparts as soon as his eyes could focus and his coordination permitted it. Frodo was plainly horrified by this development, diligently picking Brandy up by the scruff of his neck, as all cats do, and plunking him back in the box. But his revolving escapes eventually persuaded her to abandon the effort. He began to bounce around the one-bedroom apartment with reckless abandon. Climbing curtains with the nonretractable claws of a kitten was a favorite hobby.

Take that, landlady.

Frodo proved to be a terrific mother, just as Dr. Biles had said. Two delightful episodes showed her maternal instincts. The first life skill was taught when Brandy was still nursing—just a wee lad determined to climb that lumpy sofa for the first time.

Frodo had jumped up to snuggle as I was sitting on the sofa watching the small number of available free channels on the twelve-inch television brought with me from South Dakota.

Brandy watched with fascination as his mother performed this stupendous feat. In his head was the cat equivalent of the storyline in the children's book about the little blue engine: "I think I can, I think I can." He stood right next to the couch. Frodo and I could see what he planned to do, and we watched the drama unfold. Brandy paused momentarily to gather his strength and to measure the distance to the couch. He took a quick breath. He recklessly hurled himself through the air with great bravado. Had he been a crusader in Jerusalem many centuries earlier, he would have at that moment screamed out, "God wills it!"

Disappointment followed.

Brandy came straight down, exactly where his paws had left the floor. Yes, he had leapt high like a pole-vaulter, but not forward like a long jumper. A second try entangled his nonretractable claws in the bottom inch of the couch. A noble effort, to be sure, but less than successful, resulting in a gray-and-white heap on the floor. Maybe God didn't will this. His third effort finally caught the front of the couch with both front claws, and gleefully he scaled the heights. He never quit after that, climbing furniture and curtains and clothes initially, but progressing to wooden windowsills in later years at an apartment that was actually quite nice. His climbing became less amusing and more costly over time.

Frodo also taught him the virtues of imbibing a saucer of milk. She received that treat from the beginning, and although she grew more than a bit particular about it in later years, at this point she just lapped it up. One wonderful morning, when Brandy was mobile and nearly weaned, he followed her into the kitchen. I placed the saucer of milk on the floor, and Frodo promptly indulged. Brandy stood a few inches away, watching his mom with a steady gaze, his tongue lolling around just like his mother's, even though he had not yet sampled the treat. As he stepped forward, I paused to watch, sort of like the parent who wants to see their kid's first step. A seemingly endless string of tongue laps followed, but Brandy's head wasn't tipped down quite far enough. He kept missing the milk by a short distance for what seemed like an eternity, even allowing for the abundance of caution that cats exercise around liquids. I was amused even after he figured it out. Frodo was much too busy cleaning her coat to pay attention to either of us.

Grooming was a glaring fault of Frodo's mothering style. Her personal habits were impeccable—constant baths restored her soft white fur to its original luster. The pretext could be anything, from a trip outdoors to eating or drinking, to restoring her original scent after an affectionate mauling by her owner. The problem was carrying over those prodigious habits to her litter. Unfortunately for Brandy, he *was* the litter. I surmised that cats possess an instinct to clean and groom numerous kittens, because Frodo bathed him so often that he had no realistic chance of ever drying out. Brandy hunkered down when the tongue baths began, trying to shield his head by moving it around, for there she focused her tireless efforts. But he always lost the battle to duck and cover. His head was like a perpetual soggy spit wad.

Relief did not come until he learned to groom himself. Taking a cue from his mother, he cleaned himself with incredible intensity—

too much, in fact. Later in life, Brandy was diagnosed by a vet with a case of neurodermatitis, a nervous condition that includes too much grooming, leading to fur loss and bald spots. This is apparently a common problem for male cats that live too long with their mothers. Excessive grooming becomes the nervous submissive response to living in the same house as a theoretically dominant parent.

My unspoken reaction to Brandy's diagnosis went something like this: "Yeah, sure, he has a psychosomatic cat condition. And I'm Bugs Bunny." His excessive grooming was more likely the result of his earliest days as a saliva receptor.

Frodo's other fault as a mother was failing to wean Brandy in a timely fashion. Brandy was still nursing when he was nearly as large as his mother. I learned later that this behavior is common for mother cats with a solitary kitten, a reflection of the fact that they don't have the same urge to reclaim their independence and distance from their offspring. Perhaps some human intervention would have been helpful on this matter, but single men in their late twenties don't intercede in lactation issues. Not ever.

Brandy never understood the sudden shift from being nursed to being swatted away, a change that occurred without warning. I think he felt persecuted. After all, he had no siblings to reassure him that he wasn't being singled out. Life seemed arbitrary.

* * *

The two kitties met their human grandparents when I headed back to South Dakota not long after Brandy's birth. Yes, the long trek back required gasoline far in excess of my usual allotment, but this cost was offset by a full week's worth of free laundry, free food, and parental reassurance—and on the side, a few larger-denomination bills that my mom had squirreled away to slip me. The vet assured me that both cats were ready to travel, so there was no issue with taking them along. Frodo was doing exceptionally well, recovering nicely from that tough birthing process.

Our entourage headed straight north from Norman toward Sioux Falls, about a twelve-hour drive from start to finish. Frodo hopped back and forth between her two guys, joining me in the front seat and then settling down with Brandy in the box in the backseat. Brandy was mostly comatose during the long ride.

My parents—Kenneth and Verona Moen—are easily among the dearest people in the world, and they welcomed the three merry travelers with open arms, although I suspect that lengthy discussions about climbing cats preceded our arrival. Frodo entered this new place cautiously, out of fear for herself and her kitten. But once she systematically combed through the house a few times, she seemed to relax. *I've moved up in the world a notch*, she probably thought. *My plans to make something respectable of this goober appear to be working. I am a brilliant strategist.*

Brandy was put in the basement bedroom where I always slept, partly to shield him at such a tender age from the coming stream of visitors, but also to give the three of us some continuity as room-mates. The basement seemed good to the parents, too.

At first, Frodo mostly stayed downstairs with him. But before too long, she started splitting her time, opting for some human companionship upstairs. We felt sorry for little Brandy, and so we began bringing him up the stairs to be around us. Frodo tolerated the relocation, but the moment we left Brandy standing alone, she grabbed him by the scruff of his neck and raced him back down the steps. His hindquarters bounced all the way down the steep basement steps. Such indignity. Smacking your ass as you dangle helplessly from your mother's jaws is no way to go through life.

Once she got downstairs, Frodo stuck him back underneath the bed. No doubt she was struck by the sheer novelty of a spring and mattress high off the floor, providing sufficient clearance and a safe hiding spot. *Whoa, helluvan idea, this bed frame thing,* she probably thought. *Maybe the oaf will get us one of these someday.*

The cats were very comfortable in this setting, and a repeat visit some months later at Christmas only confirmed the desirability of staying here. The Christmas visit in particular provided the kitties with a whole range of new sensory experiences. The enveloping warmth of a roaring fire was especially welcome. Frodo sucked the heat up like a sponge. Pounce cat treats were an epicurean delight. The floors were lushly carpeted, and the rooms much more numerous. The only thing Frodo rejected in my mom and dad's house was the cat scratching post. She rightly concluded that it was dramatically inferior to the lumpy sofa back home, which was designed expressly for claw sharpening.

Mom tried enticing Frodo on multiple occasions to use the scratching post, hoping to save her own furnishings. But she purchased a cat scratching post that was much too small, prone to tipping. When Mom encouraged her, Frodo shot back a look that said, "Hey, you like it so much, you use it. This thing is for midget cats."

Surely, the greatest sensory experience of the holiday season was sniffing a Norway pine right there in the middle of the living room. The very idea of bringing a live tree inside was splendid in Frodo's mind, not to mention the shiny Christmas balls within paw's reach. This was a cat's Las Vegas, particularly so once presents were set underneath the tree. Every nook and cranny had to be explored. Frodo spent a joyous time in the Great Plains, sharing one of the happiest holidays of my life.

5

The Other Woman

TWO YEARS BEFORE FRODO walked into my life in Oklahoma, Donna Shalley flew into it. We first met on a late-night United Airlines flight from Chicago to Oklahoma City. I was returning from Washington, DC, where I had finished interviewing at the national headquarters of the American Political Science Association. Wedged between my soon-to-be completed PhD coursework and writing a dissertation, the interview was part of qualifying for a prestigious congressional fellowship program on Capitol Hill. The risk of failure was low because of my solid endorsement from the Carl Albert Center, but the interview itself seemed intense to a Midwestern kid who had never before set foot in the nation's capital. Hard questions posed by Fred—the sherry-sipping professor from the nearby Johns Hopkins School of Advanced International Studies, long affiliated with the Congressional Fellowship Program—slightly frazzled me.

But I was flying high both literally and figuratively on the United flight home. Before leaving town, I had learned directly from Fred—

over a glass of sherry, which I loathed but drank in solidarity—that I would be welcomed into the new class of congressional fellows.

Donna was a nursing student at Winona State University in Winona, Minnesota. Her mom lived in the Minneapolis suburbs, and Donna had hopped a plane from Minneapolis to Chicago, where she was catching the same late-night connection as me to Oklahoma City. She was meeting relatives there and the next day driving with them to Fort Smith, Arkansas, where she would stay with her dad.

Just who chased after whom on the airplane remains a controversy to this very day.

Her version is that I actually initiated conversation between the two of us and rather boldly asked to exchange addresses before the airplane taxied to the gate in Oklahoma City. All of that is true.

But I believe my side of this dispute is more convincing. I boarded well in advance of Donna, sitting in my duly assigned seat many rows back on a virtually empty airplane. In those days, airlines flew the planes whether or not there were many passengers, so late-night, cheaper flights were sometimes almost empty. So there I was, sitting happily in my aisle seat to stretch out my legs on a virtually empty plane, with my tray down to rest my book upon, waiting for the few remaining laggards to get aboard and be seated.

Donna the laggard comes marching past empty seat after empty seat and row after row. She stops right next to me and says, "Excuse me, but I have that window seat." She points to it. I look up from my book, seeing nothing but endless numbers of empty seats in every possible direction for 360 degrees. Probably muttering under my breath, I'm thinking to myself, *Really, lady, you want me to close my tray, unbuckle my seat belt, kick my bag even farther under the seat in front of me, and stand up and move into the aisle so that you can slip past me here in row twenty-two, as opposed to sitting in any of the fifteen available seats within tobacco-spitting distance? Is that it?*

Guess so, I thought, as she continued hovering. So I went through those oh-so-many steps to let her into the window seat. We had an empty middle seat, as did every row in the airplane.

She sat down and struggled mightily to remove her jacket. At this point, the natural male response kicked in to catch a few glances as this lovely young woman started peeling off her outerwear. Young men often glance at young women's clothing adjustments, maybe to see if they'll need to be gallant, but perhaps for reasons that are not quite so gentlemanly. They secretly dream that this will be that one time in a billion when the disrobing young woman turns to them and sultrily says, "Hey, big boy, feast your eyes on this." Young men living in the Candy Loving era at OU were especially vulnerable to this line of flawed thinking.

My deep-set, squinty little eyes widened as this woman slowly disrobed. But much to my disappointment, she stopped right after the outerwear. Oh well, she was an attractive lass, and now that I was tuned in a bit, this seemed to be an encouraging situation. Here we have a perfectly empty airplane, and this doll makes it a point to march past all of those empty seats and rows in order to sit right next to me?

Babycakes must really want me to flirt with her.

Hell, it all made perfect sense to me. I was a little older, highly educated, a devilishly good-looking chap, fit as an Olympian, and obviously going places. And while she might not have known all of that when she absolutely insisted on sitting next to me, the chances were good that I was exuding some masculine power and wisdom en route back from the corridors of power in the nation's capital. Women can just sense men like me, I figured.

Of course, the mind-numbing drugs could have played a part in her decision. Donna was a beleaguered woman when we met up on that United flight. Several days prior, she had undergone major shoulder surgery. She sported a sling and possessed intense painkillers. She was palpably uncomfortable. Her trouble getting off her jacket was due to having only one functioning arm.

Drugs impairing her judgment worked to my distinct advantage, no question. To this day, she claims not to remember much about the flight or our conversation, thus feeding the flames of controversy about who chased whom in the airplane.

Personally, I think she remains sore that she was but a practice run for my later rescue of the homeless little white kitty in distress. If that thought had never occurred to her, I regret mentioning it in this book.

Anyway, I made a good first impression. By asking her why she was on the flight to Oklahoma City, I gained the pretext to mention that I was returning from Washington, DC, where I would be moving in a few months to work for Congress.

"Yes, I'll be working right on Capitol Hill. It's all part of my PhD program and my future plans as a tenured university professor," I dribbled out. "Or didn't I mention that I was finishing up my doctorate?"

After planting those seeds, I bent down and dug out my bag from beneath the seat in front of me. I began rummaging through it, as if looking for some vital documents, possibly from the Speaker of the House, befitting my role as someone who would be helping to run the nation. Never mind that there were thousands of employees on Capitol Hill already, most of them gainfully employed rather than working temporarily as congressional fellows. Never mind that the only things in my briefcase were souvenir pamphlets. She was none the wiser so long as I carefully left everything inside the bag while rummaging through it.

Second impression? Not so good.

I had established en route to Oklahoma City (as Donna faded in and out of consciousness) that there was no particular woman in my life. This is an observation that single men often like to relay, even though single women don't ever inquire. This time, I tried to frame it as being too busy with the life of the mind, too concerned with the plight of a desperate world, to have time for dating.

Unfortunately, while I was making small talk with Donna as we entered the terminal at Will Rogers Airport in Oklahoma City, I was unexpectedly embraced by a buxom blonde who cheerfully said, "Hi Matt, welcome back."

I stammered an awkward hello. At the same instant, Donna started sliding away from me. Her body language said it all: "No girlfriend and finishing up a doctorate? What a pig."

My roommate at the time, Doc, had double-parked outside the empty terminal at this late hour and sent his future wife, Jan, into the terminal to retrieve me. That's all it was.

Seeing Donna slipping away, I brushed off Jan a bit and tried to reengage. But a hug from a babe was hard to overcome in the terminal of an airport. "Are you all set?" I managed to ask Donna. She replied a bit coldly that her relatives were not here yet, but they would be along soon, so I was free to go on my way. *Ouch.* We said good-bye and promised to write, but it seemed to be only a polite gesture on her part.

Obviously, I should have handled that better. But it wasn't easy. Here was the monologue that would have had to happen: "Donna, please meet Jan. She is not my girlfriend because I don't have a girlfriend. She is my buddy's girlfriend. I don't actually know where he is at the moment, but I am sure there is a very good explanation. She probably just met me here at the airport, and while he doesn't seem to be here, I'm sure he will be along soon. And just so you know, Jan hugged me because she hadn't seen me for a while. And Doc wouldn't mind this, wherever he is at this late hour, because the two of them are the item, not the two of us."

You get the picture. But try that one in an airport terminal where everyone is scattering to the winds. Having obtained her address before we taxied to the gate, I just accepted Donna's polite promise to write and walked off with Jan.

My third impression was stellar.

After getting out to the car and loading my luggage curbside, I asked Doc to wait a minute while I ran back inside the terminal. I wanted to make sure that Donna was not alone in an unfamiliar city, taking pain medication, with her arm in a sling. She was still standing at the deserted arrival gate, awaiting her relatives. She seemed pleased to see me. Yes, I was still very much a pig, but at least a familiar pig.

This return visit without Jan at my side offered me the opportunity to fully explain. "Donna," I suggested, "how about you and I make our way down to the baggage claim area before your luggage disappears, and maybe we'll encounter your relatives?" She accepted this sensible plan, and as we walked through the airport together, we schmoozed a bit. More alert as we sauntered, she proved to be excellent company. It turned out her relatives weren't all that familiar with the traditional airport protocol of the time. Sure enough, we found them as we neared the luggage carousel.

We said good-bye a second time and both promised to write. There was some conviction in her voice this time, and she did actually write first, proving all along that she was the one chasing me. We wrote many letters and visited each other in Minnesota and Washington, DC, over the course of the next couple of years. Interregnums occurred in our relationship, but our destiny was cutely sealed on an airline named United.

* * *

Transfixed over the telephone by Frodo's birthing story, Donna was now following through with the solo driving trip to see her dad—that trip where I wasn't sure whether I was a rest stop or a destination. She loaded up her Ford Escort and drove down from Minnesota to Oklahoma.

I hitched my pants up a bit and, feeling smug, thought: *Yeah, she is pretty much coming to see me, no matter what she may claim. The route to Arkansas from Minnesota does not pass through the state of Oklahoma.* Of course, lingering in the back of my mind was the worry that stopping to see me was just the Persian cat lover's ruse to personally meet the C-sectioned white cat.

True cat lovers will stop at nothing.

"Frodo!" Donna exclaimed with great enthusiasm upon entering my apartment. "How are you? It is nice to meet you. I've heard so much about you." She swept up my little white princess into her arms to affectionately rub her chin. Standard procedure for a cat lover.

Whoa! thought Frodo. *Back right up, you miserable wench.*

What an egregious violation of protocol. No bending down, no extending her fingers, no submitting to kitty cat sniffing privileges. Just some sort of weird raptor behavior from this Minnesota woman, this business of swooping down without warning and picking up an innocent victim. *Back home, she probably has a job at the zoo feeding mice to the eagles,* Frodo probably thought.

Frodo pushed away. Once she was set down, the obviously miffed cat moved several paces away before plunking down. She shot a look back to Donna that said, "Who in the hell are you? Who invited you here? And just where on earth did you learn your manners, at a cage fight?"

You could tell by her kitty facial expression exactly what she was thinking: *Anyone who enters a room that way is a dimwit who will never amount to much.*

Donna exacerbated this tense situation by quickly foisting upon us pictures of Lacey, her most recently acquired Persian. Having just met Frodo, she reasoned we would want to meet Lacey.

Talking about misreading a situation.

Yes, I smiled and cooed over the flat-faced wonder, but only because I calculated that a positive response was more likely to keep open the possibility of some late-night whoopee. Secretly, I thought to myself, *Three hundred and fifty bucks for a prissy Persian… and it doesn't hold a candle to my beloved Frodo. Probably dumber than a stump. No room in that flat head for any brains.*

My little white princess may not have followed the entire conversation, but she obviously sensed that this intruder was promoting some rival cat. Protocol violation number two, with still more likely to follow. I naturally interpreted Frodo's utter indifference to the cooing over Lacey as her way of coping with deep hurt. It seemed more plausible to Frodo's biggest fan than the idea that she just wasn't paying very close attention.

All I can say is that it's lucky that I was in the room, or there could've been an old-fashioned catfight between the two- and four-legged females standing toe-to-paw in my living room.

But even though my two gals started off on the wrong foot, they quickly established a genuine friendship over the course of the week. For her part, Donna accepted the protocol of the sniff and rubby. She diligently brushed Frodo; performed tummy rubs, chin rubs, and ear scratches; and most importantly, introduced delectable moist cat food into the house. This new taste enthralled Frodo, who must have wondered where this stuff had been hidden in the apartment. She acted as if canned cat food was a precious and rare commodity, not a gravy-packed, skunk-smelling selection of discarded animal parts. As she grew accustomed to its availability, she became somewhat more demanding and selective about the flavor du jour. Beef was only a top twenty hit, for instance, while chicken was top ten, and liver topped the charts.

Frodo reached out to Donna in return. She agreed to the sniff and rubby, consented to be brushed, accepted the tummy and chin rubs and ear scratches, and enthusiastically began eating all of the totally scrumptious smelly food that was laid before her. In a cat's mind, this is meeting a human more than halfway.

One day that week, the kind of intense thunderstorm that rips through Oklahoma every so often in the spring knocked out power to almost the entire city of Norman. With nowhere to go, we stayed in the apartment, and I taught Donna how to play backgammon. Frodo was intrigued by a board game played on the floor. She sat next to me as Donna and I took turns moving shiny tokens. Even better, the tokens moved only after the dice rolled all the way across the board. Good god—utterly random, occasional movement! Frodo watched this game intently, as if trying to learn it. She occasionally tapped a dropped die with her paw, or moved the tokens around.

I joked that Frodo was grasping the essentials, confident that she would pick up the fine points later. Donna was less optimistic, laughing at Frodo's earnest involvement and dropping sarcastic comments about the dumb blonde. While I cannot claim with certitude that Frodo learned backgammon, she provided a delightful memory and a lasting legacy. Her white cat fur stuck to the felt backgammon board like Velcro. Strands from the Era of the White Fur remained embedded for years, preserved like the DNA samples of the mastodons that slid into the La Brea tar pits in Los Angeles.

Brandy's activities during the week of Donna's visit are a blur. Using the lexicon of modern childrearing, he was constantly acting out and literally impossible to restrain. To me, this was more telling evidence that he was switched at birth. His most demonic performance was shredding an entire box of tissues into the tiniest of pieces throughout the whole length and breadth of the living room.

Donna and I awoke to a certifiable tissue massacre. Cats lack the facial muscles that allow dogs to be so expressive, but I swear that Frodo's face read: "No, not my kid. Grown up now. You two handle it." Donna and I picked up tiny bits of tissue off the floor for a very long time, appreciating only the fact that Brandy was now too exhausted to be annoying to us. His digestive tract was probably busy processing pulp.

Donna and I parted company amidst great sadness at the end of that week. Frodo had been an inadvertent foil, a friend, and a companion to both of us. We chuckled at her antics. We brought her treats. We admired her manner, especially in comparison to her hellish son. I think we actually grew closer because of her. For the first time since we'd met on that United Airlines flight to Oklahoma City, we broached the subject of spending our lives together.

6

Harebrained

NOT TOO LONG AFTER Donna's visit to Norman, I completed an oral defense of my dissertation and was henceforth eligible to be called Dr. Moen. The thesis defense was an engaging, pleasant affair. I passed with highest honors, won a dissertation award, and received some excellent advice from committee members, including the one whose ankles had been targeted. Eventually, this work became the basis for my first published book.

Counting the fellowship stint on Capitol Hill, six years of my life had passed since I'd first moved to Norman to begin my graduate work. Quiet years mostly, while I incrementally picked up a master's degree, a doctorate, a white cat, and the white cat's wild son. Humans found the educational progress impressive and knew that it was time for me to move on; the cats cared little about any of the progress and opposed the move.

Moving is patently offensive to cats because it interrupts routine. Each day in the life of a cat is spent rehearsing and practicing routine, based on the principle that routine is the equivalent of the Buddhist nirvana. Cats must think it so because they take routine so very seriously. Even moving the same household furnishings around the same space is a poor idea in a cat's mind. The ideal is the permanency of Stonehenge or the Great Pyramid.

But the time had come. I was all done being a graduate student, part-time teacher, Sooner football fan, and the steady boyfriend of Candy Loving. Well, okay, perhaps that last part reflects my poor memory or vivid imagination.

Writing off my one month's deposit from Ashley Square seemed a given, particularly because the landlady didn't walk through the apartment with departing renters as they turned in their keys. She just thanked me for being part of the apartment family and said she would be sure to send along any refund that I was due after her team entered the apartment and assessed the situation.

"You see," she said, "there are just so many things we do not know, like whether we will have to clean carpets or do some repairs. And there are so many apartments that we are responsible for in this complex. We have a team of qualified specialists who can make these determinations for us."

"But I'll be in South Dakota by then," I protested. "I finally finished up my academic program here at OU, so I won't be coming back if there are any questions or issues."

You could almost see the gleam in her eye and hear the snicker in her throat. Twenty-three years of my life in school practicing critical thinking, and still I was naive enough to let on that I was going to be gone, gone, gone forever. *Matt, you foolish, foolish man*, I thought to myself right after the words about my permanent departure slipped out.

My parents came down to Norman to help with the move. They had visited only once during my six years there, partly because I often journeyed back home to South Dakota, but also to instill the lesson that I was officially on my own in this world. Mom would have come more often, but Dad was orphaned as a kid and grew up well adjusted with a little tough love and a lot of independence. He figured his son ought to do the same. A reasonable thought from a terrific dad.

All of my worldly possessions fit quite easily into two cars. I owned mostly books and little else. The only unexpected twist to packing was adding in one small table that had come into my possession in a roundabout, furniture-swapping, leftover sort of way at Ashley Square; it seemed as though the apartment complex would want me to have it if they were going to end up keeping my deposit.

Frodo didn't approve of any of this nonsense. She had been happy and amused when my parents showed up, consistent with her genuine affection for people. But this business of uprooting and leaving the only place that she might have ever really called home, for some unknown reason and distant destination ... well, why wouldn't she be shattered? We had started a life together here. And it had its perks. The next-door neighbor had proved so hospitable that he kept a litter box for Frodo in his apartment, along with a little cat food. When his deck door was open, she was welcome to saunter in and do as she pleased. This was a level of neighborliness that not even old-time television staples Ricky and Lucy enjoyed with Fred and Ethel. Jeff the friendly neighbor was forever telling me about his plans to leave OU and travel across Europe with a backpack sporting a very large Canadian flag to throw off the anti-American crowd overseas.

Frodo became downright agitated as we continued packing. *What is this? Why are we doing this? What in the world is happening? Why are we leaving our home?*

Out of fear that they might run off while we were loading up, we locked Frodo and Brandy in the bathroom. Frodo was used to having the run of the place (no doors closed, thank you). To first see the sights and then hear the sounds of moving while being locked behind a door was terribly distressing. For all she knew, I could be walking out on her, as might have happened to her earlier in life. She was always too friendly and warm to have been a feral cat. Her distressed cries emanating from behind the bathroom door broke my heart. Brandy sensed his mom's genuine anxiety and nervously clammed up. Their familiar world was collapsing.

By this time, I probably should have parted with Brandy for his own good. It would have ended his inner turmoil over being the subservient household cat, when nature told him he was rightly the dominant cat. I think Frodo would have happily packed his bags, figuring that a new foster home might help his behavior. But it was impossible to part with that bad little boy—Frodo's only son. No one else would easily have tolerated him, and no new owner could ever fully grasp and appreciate his rocky entrance into this world.

For the first two hours on the road, my beloved white princess wailed endlessly. I felt like the Tin Man in *The Wizard of Oz*, who stated that he knew he had a heart because it was breaking. Frodo was absolutely inconsolable. She would stand up, lie down, stand up again and gaze out the windows, move from the front to the back seat, and then start all over again. She would step on my lap and look out the window while I was driving, all the while voicing her intense displeasure at this unexpected turn of events. No amount of petting or reassurance comforted her. Not until the Kansas border did she reconcile herself to the situation.

Packing and farewells having taken a while, we got a late start and drove only as far as Topeka, Kansas, before calling it a night. We were past halfway, we reasoned, and we might as well pull in before it grew any later. We checked into an economy hotel, where we were given a second-floor room that was going to hold three people and two smuggled cats banned by policy from staying in the hotel. The smuggling operation was relatively easy—placing the cats into a cardboard box with a jacket tossed over it proved sufficient to get them into the room. The only unexpected twist to this furtive operation was Frodo's high anxiety. In addition to yowling from inside the box as I walked her into the hotel through the side entrance, the unhappy cat managed to leap straight out of the box, staging a clean getaway as she raced down a long hall in the direction of the front desk.

Mom and I immediately gave chase, laughing a bit at this sordid affair but worried that either the hotel manager would send us packing with no refund or the much beloved Frodo, like Houdini, would somehow manage to escape. Since she wasn't at all sure of her flight path or final destination, Frodo hesitated twice as she sped down the hallway. But like a toddler, she accelerated when we closed the gap. She was just about to round the corner and head down the short hallway toward the front desk when I caught and scooped up the runaway, even less ceremoniously than Donna had the first time the two of them met.

"Gotcha, Frodo," I whispered to her. "What do you think you are doing, anyway?" She might have plausibly asked me the same question.

Relieved, I speedily whisked her into the hotel room. Careful to stick our foot in the door opening to push her back into the room as we made several subsequent trips to the car to bring in the night's essentials, we finished the job. Celebrating my years in Norman, and the graduation exercises that I was destined to miss by virtue of my relocation, we headed out on the town for dinner on Dad. I don't know why we worried so much about the presence of the kitty cats in the hotel. Pulling back into the parking lot after dinner, we spied the two cats standing proudly side by side in the window of the second-floor room, looking down at the parking lot and at a major portion of Topeka too. They were visible for miles around.

* * *

Ah, to be back home again. Free lodging, free food, laundry services, more space, a fishing boat, and very few cares in the world—the good life. I lapped up the congratulations of relatives and old friends who stopped by, grinning upon hearing the Dr. Moen salutation. But perhaps best of all that summer were built-in babysitters for Frodo and Brandy when I jumped into my car and headed off to see Donna, who had graduated with a bachelor of science in nursing from Winona State. She was living with her mom in the Minneapolis area, working at Mercy Hospital. Five hours apart was the closest we had ever lived. It seemed like a breeze.

Proud of my accomplishments, and terrific parents then and always, Mom and Dad happily let me sponge off them and use their home as a base of operations for the rest of the summer.

Whether Frodo remembered the house from our prior Christmas visit is unknown. Do cats recall a physical place months later? Does the furniture or the traffic pattern ring a bell? What about the smell? Any faint, lingering cat odors to remind them of their stay?

Brandy probably remembered bouncing his ass on the hard steps to the basement as his momma took him back down to stow him under the bed. I suspect he was glad to be his own autonomous being this time around.

Whether or not the cats remembered, they adjusted quickly to the new surroundings. They enjoyed more people around to meet their needs. They relished the numerous and fine furnishings. And the backyard was full of trees, which were full of birds.

Ah, birds. Too damn bad they knew how to fly.

Having finished my degree, I was a happy and relaxed fellow. The only rub was that I was often away in Minneapolis with that other female, the one who was actually turning out to amount to something, despite Frodo's earlier predictions. Traveling to meet up fell to me most of the time because she was a relatively new, place-bound hospital employee. By contrast, I was, uh, sort of unemployed, confirming Frodo's initial take on me.

"It's okay, Frodo," I would explain to her. "I'll be back in a few days."

If she sensed the intrusion of another female, she didn't let on. She knew my heart had a spot reserved expressly for her.

What a unique few months for me. I was feeling accomplished and carefree, and I had a female wanting to share my life on each end of my travels between Sioux Falls and Minneapolis. Contentment is the only word that comes close to describing it.

* * *

Summer was less serene for my parents, who had every right to expect that their youngest son wouldn't be back living in their house at his age, let alone with two climbing felines in tow. Mom resurrected the notion that the kitties would like to use the miniature scratching post she had purchased for them the last time they visited.

"Oh, no thanks," the kitties seemed to say. "We're used to having free reign to scratch up the household furnishings. We like couches best. They are heavy, with strong threads."

Most of the time, my folks accepted their role as surrogate grandparents with gracious good humor. This was especially true with Frodo, who spent most of her days happily ensconced in the backyard bushes, waiting for the one special bird that decided to walk rather than fly over to my dad's elevated birdfeeder. "Always hopeful" is probably the best way to describe it.

Brandy? He engaged in what is traditionally called hooliganism.

Incident number one occurred on a sunny South Dakota day. Dad and I were sitting on the matching patio chairs, watching Frodo romp aimlessly among the backyard flowers and plants. She was switching between hiding, crouching, twitching, and pouncing. Anything that *might* move drew her interest. Mom, on the other hand, was standing by herself at the kitchen sink, fixing dinner and intermittently glancing out the window above the sink. We occupied opposite sides of the house.

We hadn't been out on the patio for long before my mom marched straight out to make a pronouncement. Her knees were still knocking, and she was nervously laughing.

"Do you know what *your* cat just did?" she asked me.

Uh-oh. *My* cat. This couldn't be good.

I could see Frodo in the backyard doing nothing troublesome, thus narrowing the list of possible culprits. Sorely tempted to lighten the moment, I wanted to point at Frodo and reply, "Uh, not much, Mom." But I sensed that my dinner hinged on playing it straight, so I gently inquired, "No, what happened?"

"Well, let me just tell you," she said as she plopped down on a patio step to stop the knee-knocking. "I was standing right at the kitchen window when *your* cat jumped straight up from the driveway and glommed on to the screen. It's six feet off the ground! He scared the daylights out of me, with his little beady eyes looking right in at me, the *dumb bunny*."

Oh no. "Dumb bunny" was about the most serious utterance that one ever heard from my mother. As children, we dreaded being called the proverbial dumb bunny because it meant we had seriously screwed up. My fun-loving older brother, Mike, qualified as a dumb bunny the time he knocked over the gallon of oil-based house paint while high up on scaffolding; its off-white color hit not only the house and concrete driveway but also my mother's clothes and hair. This topped my sweet sister Rose Ann's sunbathing episode on top of the garage, which resulted in her rolling off, happily unhurt. Mom saved up "dumb bunny" for such significant events.

Both Dad and I burst out laughing uproariously at the thought of Brandy's six-foot-high leap, leading to Mom's one-foot-high leap. But even funnier to me was the thought that Brandy's feet might have touched back down to earth before my mom's. Wisely, I kept that innermost man thought to myself.

"Well, sorry to hear it, Mom," I said. This wasn't exactly the apology for my cat's bad behavior that she was seeking, but I figured it split the difference by acknowledging an unfortunate incident. Quickly realizing that this was the most sympathy she was going to receive from her two giggling dumb bunnies, Mom went back inside, probably weighing for the first time in her life whether or not to spit in our food.

Dad and I exchanged a quick glance once she left, which naturally caused us to start laughing all over again. Men sometimes think stuff is doubly funny when women don't think it is funny at all. The Three Stooges are the most cited example. We figured no one had been injured and Brandy was just being himself. The retelling triggered even more laughter.

After we finally quieted down, my dad made a solemn announcement indicative of a life spent in the Great Plains: "Your four-legged wonder probably put holes in the kitchen screen big enough for mosquitoes to fit through. And we have a lot of mosquitoes."

A practical consideration. Practical people, these Midwesterners. Especially true for people like my parents, born early enough to remember the Dust Bowl days when swarms of grasshoppers actually ate the fence posts. Practicality contributed to their being among our country's greatest citizens, for they've always moved ahead without complaint.

So I had to agree with Dad. Mosquito holes were bad. But secretly, I was proud. My one-year-old boy had leapt six feet straight up, the kitty equivalent of the triple Salchow jump in figure skating! Just months earlier, he had tried twice to climb the lumpy sofa in the Ashley Square apartment before succeeding. Now he was one of the Flying Wallendas, an acrobat capable of defying the heights with the greatest of ease. My boy had panache.

Incident number two turned the tables on my dad, irritating him at least as much as incident number one had bothered my mom. It happened while I was in Minneapolis, visiting Donna, and it ultimately involved mosquitoes, but on a much grander scale.

Mom and Dad were, and are, regular parishioners of Our Savior's Lutheran Church. They were among the charter members of what over time came to be one of the largest and most influential Lutheran congregations in Sioux Falls, with something like 4,000 members. Located straight across the street from Augustana College, the church was where all four of their children were baptized, confirmed, and forced to sing against their will in the church youth choir. For more than half a century, my parents have lived out the Lutheran creed of salvation through grace.

The incident happened on an otherwise pleasant Sunday morning. Running a little bit late for church, they hurriedly tried to locate the two kitties before heading out. All summer long, the kitties enjoyed outdoor privileges during daylight hours. We always ushered them inside by day's end, so we knew they were safe and so they would remain daytime companions rather than nocturnal roamers. Mom and Dad were extra vigilant about keeping the kitties safe when I was gone, for the obvious reason that they didn't want something to happen on their watch.

They spotted Frodo on the living-room floor, fast asleep. Brandy had been let out over an early-morning cup of coffee, and now he was nowhere to be found. Mom and Dad say they both went outside in their Sunday best, calling Brandy and poking at the backyard bushes and flowers in a vain attempt to round him up.

They investigated. They dithered. I had impressed upon them the need for the kitties to be safely inside whenever everyone was gone. While their backyard was safe, their front yard abutted a busy street. Dad apparently argued that Brandy would be just fine on his own for one lousy hour of the morning, since he had been outside so many times without incident. Mom reluctantly agreed. At least this was the bad boy rather than the white princess.

Returning home an hour later, they spied Brandy resting comfortably on the living-room sofa. Hmm, perplexing. Hadn't he been outside? Mom and Dad concluded that Brandy had slipped back into the house without them noticing, a distinct possibility since cats are the very definition of stealth.

Then Dad's eyes fixated on the answer to the riddle. I am only guessing that his head tilted just a little bit to the side at that point, just as a cat that's about to fight falls on its back so that it has all of its claws available. The glass door having been left open on a beautiful sunny day in a place where there isn't much crime, the patio screen door now had one perfectly cat-sized hole right through it. Brandy had carved a personal cat door. It seemed to me that this was an eminently practical solution to the problem of being outdoors while wanting indoors, but that was not how my dad saw it.

Had I listened carefully while in Minneapolis, I probably could have heard the actual words: "*Brandyyy*, you little %$#*&."

Dad didn't always settle for the phrase "dumb bunny."

Brandy loved this new passageway. He suddenly felt the freedom of Columbus or Magellan, for they too were unfettered explorers of the big world. The carved cat door was just the right height and width to fit him. It allowed for much coming and going, entry and exit. It connected the comfortable furniture of the living room with the patio steps leading to the great outdoors. What a magnificent location for a door.

Truthfully, we never quite figured out why he did it. Did he panic outside? Was he just bored? Was he hungry? Was he lonesome for his mom or human companions? Regardless of the reason, I can tell you with certainty that compared to the small rips in the kitchen screen, the deck screen now held the queen mother of all mosquito holes.

"Hey, Dad," I wanted to say when I returned from Minneapolis, "you really don't need to worry anymore about those little holes in the kitchen screen." Only fear of personal safety restrained me.

To this day, Dad good-naturedly reminds me about the rampaging cat that attacked his home to get inside rather than out. He continuously mentions that the door doesn't work well because the replacement screen (which he bought himself) is stretched too tight. Maybe I should have had Brandy loosen it up at some point.

Frodo stayed out of trouble the entire summer. No trips to the vet for fleas or injuries. Three loving humans constantly pampering her, along with the other woman when she came to Sioux Falls for a couple of long weekends. A wayward son striking out on his own, freeing her of the responsibilities of motherhood. A burgeoning collection of cat toys, given by well-wishers and visitors to the house. A backyard filled with birds and beasts and flowers. And yes, a guy she loved to share a cool basement with on those warm summer nights.

* * *

Over dinner in a restaurant at the St. Anthony Main complex in downtown Minneapolis, Donna and I sealed our future plans. Before finishing my dissertation defense, I had accepted a job as an assistant professor of political science at the University of Maine. I had to be there by September 1 for the start of classes. We literally pulled out a calendar, looked at a road map to estimate the length of the drive, and settled on August 18 as the day when we would head off together to a state that neither of us had ever visited, save the two days in Orono when I interviewed at UM. I will always remember those interview days clearly. The space shuttle *Challenger* exploded during that time.

Whether I invited Donna or she invited herself depends a little on how you interpret the words spoken between us over the course of the summer. Either way, she incurred all of the risk. I was heading off to a new job to start an academic career, taking my two kitties and my mother, who wanted to go to help with the driving (she said), but who mostly wanted to be sure that we somehow landed on our feet. These logistics also made sense because her paint-dropping older son, Mike, lived with his family in Boston, so she could ride out with me, then go down to visit him.

Paint dropping is purposefully mentioned twice in this book in connection with my older brother as good-natured payback for things that all younger brothers understand.

I drove a final time from Sioux Falls to Minneapolis, where we picked up Donna and started off east through upper Wisconsin, toward the scenic Trans-Canada Highway. Lake Michigan lies squarely between Minneapolis and Maine, and a traveler may go north or south around it. We opted for the northern route for practical reasons, like avoiding Chicago and the large cities clustered along the I-80 corridor. Since it is standard practice in cat books to ascribe one's own decisions to feline influence, let me hasten to add that Frodo wanted to see the Great White North.

The start of the journey was marked by excitement, but also sadness. Left behind was a delightful summer, the safety of my home, and a loving father. Buried in Centerville, South Dakota, on the very day that I left for Minneapolis, was my Uncle Arnie, an affable man who had shelled corn in Irene, South Dakota, for most of his life before succumbing to lung cancer, probably caused by the inhalation of crop dust and pesticides over the years. I went from being a pallbearer at his funeral in Centerville to Sioux Falls to change clothes and jump into an already packed car to start east. It was a bittersweet day.

Beginning in Minneapolis, car number one in the caravan was an exceedingly high mileage Pontiac Bonneville bought from the father of a friend of mine in Sioux Falls. Part of the reason for its purchase was a generous offer of $500 on my purple AMC Gremlin by the librarian at my old high school. He needed a low-priced car for his teenage son. Five hundred bucks? After paying a dealer $1,400 for the car so many years before, I jumped on that deal. With a little cash advance from Mom and Dad, who realized that soon I would at long last be gainfully employed, I traded up to the $2,500 used Bonneville, sold to me at a fire-sale price because of my relationship with the family.

Car number two in the caravan was Donna's Ford Escort, only two years old because she was gainfully employed. What exactly did she give up for this journey? Only her well-paying job, her condominium shared with her mother, her Minnesota friends, her two Persian kitties (who stayed with her mom), and general peace of mind. Donna's sacrifice and risk-taking here is some sort of testimony to the human spirit.

So car number one, driven by me, held my mother, the two kitties, and a litter box in the backseat, along with my material possessions. Car number two held Donna and her things. Off to New England we headed together, with only a single director's chair between us. We had no other furnishings, other than a leftover table that had come my way as part of a unilateral settlement with Ashley Square.

I led and Donna followed across the length of Canada. We joked about being in the big car versus the little car. The big car had air-conditioning (a first for me), so the two kitties dozed lazily in the spacious Bonneville, either in the front or back seat. The Escort had only rolled-down windows for air, and even central Canada can be hot in mid-August. At one rest stop, an envious Donna snapped a photo of life in the big car, capturing Brandy in the middle of a telling yawn.

I wish I could regale you with merry tales about the 1,600-mile journey, but it was mostly long and wearisome, especially at the slower Canadian speed limits. Every night, we had to sneak the kitties into a hotel, usually past a sign that read "Absolutely No Pets Allowed." The smuggling process rarely went smoothly. As in Topeka, I would shove the cats into a box, toss a towel or jacket over them, and whisk them into the room. They did not appreciate that treatment one bit. They did not often voice displeasure as we passed the hotel clerks, but they often thumped around in the box. "Look straight ahead, pretend nothing is happening," I would say to myself, taking on the role of a luggage handler for an airline.

Frodo never seemed as distressed about this journey as she had been about our departure from Oklahoma. She probably assumed we were moving up again in life, wherever we were heading. And the upside of being confined to a car was food and a litter box but one step away. Comfort without effort has demonstrable appeal to cats.

Of course, part of her peace of mind came from her total trust in me. She knew from our time together that I would nurture and protect her no matter what and no matter where we went.

7

Quakers Have It All Figured Out

YEARS AGO, A BEST-SELLING book suggested that everything a person needed to know in life was learned in kindergarten. A cute but silly premise, for we learn by leaps and bounds as we age, and learning continues throughout our lives. In my case, I gleaned a few simple lessons in my late twenties and thirties by living with a white cat.

Some of these lessons are pedestrian. Frodo stopped to smell the roses—quite literally, in her case. And while that isn't exactly a novel thought, it is a good reminder to insert more unhurried minutes into the day.

Given our busy lives, we can easily fail to connect with others and to revel in their companionship. My very affectionate and loyal white cat stopped me cold on a good many occasions, insisting that she be given her due. At first I resisted—too busy. But I gradually came to cherish these unhurried minutes, and I came to think about them in just that way, softly stroking and talking to her. Following these more natural rhythms of ancestral life brought contentment.

Each Sunday morning at my church, Pastor Steve tells his parishioners to take a few minutes to let some of the outright busyness of their lives dissipate, so they might reconnect with their humanity and with God. He brings a sense of challenge and calm and is easily the most interesting minister I have encountered. But I confess that when he encourages us to let go of the frenetic pace of our lives so that we may begin thinking about God, my mind will sometimes drift back to a little white cat and some unhurried minutes.

Frodo led the way to more attentiveness. I missed early signs that she was a stray. I did not see the warning signs of her difficult labor and delivery. And I didn't initially grasp her need to sleep next to me at night for the sake of routine and safety, even when her kitten came home. These lapses flowed from inattention to unspoken needs. Perhaps there is some larger lesson that applies to children or others who are powerless in our society. We need to hear what they cannot voice.

Another lesson I learned first from my parents, but Frodo reinforced it. While money creates better circumstances, it doesn't buy true happiness. When Frodo walked into my life, I owned virtually nothing except books and a strange purple car. The worst apartment during my years in Norman didn't circulate heat in my bedroom, so I slept all of one winter in a pair of sweatpants and a stocking cap. Tevye the dairyman in *Fiddler on the Roof* resonated with me because of his observation that while it was no sin to be poor, it was no great honor either.

The point? What brought so much happiness during my tough times was a friendly cat's loving gaze, gentle purr, and presence. None of those things could be bought or rented, and they were gifts given freely to me.

Watching Frodo teach Brandy was also instructive. He looked to her for sustenance at first and then for guidance and direction. He imitated her moves, such as his awkward efforts to mimic her jump onto the couch and slurps from a saucer. Rhetoric about role models is not trite in the cat kingdom.

Frodo's contributions proceeded past being a role model. She knew when to let him go. She quit nursing him. She stopped watching out for him. She slowly let him take control of his own life. She instinctively sensed that she could nurture another's life, but could not live it, no matter how much she cared.

* * *

Frodo taught hard lessons as well. Harm sometimes comes to the innocent. Suffering occurs where it is unwarranted. Death is an occasional byproduct of attempts to create life. Proof was her struggle to deliver and the death of three of her four kittens.

In a lighter vein, Frodo structured so much of my time and so many of my choices! The standard line is that cats are supposed to take care of themselves. That's a major reason people pick cats over dogs. But just what does having a cat mean in terms of actual human commitment? How truly self-sufficient are cats?

If I had asked her, Frodo would have explained:

First and foremost, I must have food. Not just any food. It must pass my extremely close inspection, and I have one of the best sniffers on the planet. Set it down in exactly the same place as the day before. No substitutes. No sale items. Just the same stuff—the stuff I like.

Water too. Clean water, please, running out of a tap if at all possible. Only in a bowl if it's freshly poured. Nice and cold. Shower droplets I can suck off the tile are particularly tasty, so hop in and clean up, please.

Cat treats are indispensable. Top-of-the-line ones. Skip shrimp flavor. What is a shrimp anyway? Never seen one. Chicken is tasty and succulent. Keep the lid tight so the treats stay fresh.

Cat toys are extremely annoying, but a few hundred spread all around the house add to the ambiance and make the place seem cat friendly. Strings or balls only, please. No mix-and-match. Toss the squeak toys—that's dog junk.

A scratching post is a necessity, but you don't need to buy one. The sofa will do. Move it to a central location so I don't have to walk far from wherever I'm resting. A sofa that catches early-morning sun is good. Heavy-duty thread stretched tightly over a queen sleeper sofa is optimal.

And yes, I have a few incidental needs: cat furniture to lie on; a clean litter box; some lube for occasional hairballs; a taste of milk from time to time; flea and/or worm medicine; a brush (even though I don't want it used on me, unless of course, I want it used on me); a designer food bowl; a kitty carrier (but don't put me in it); a fragrant tree at Christmas time; a cat thermometer, which should not be confused with any others in the house; a favorite blanket (or expensive wardrobe item) to sleep on; a claw clipper; an Elizabethan collar for the rare mishap; cat toothpaste or a dental cat food; and odds and ends that you should be thinking of for me all of the time on your own.

This is but a partial listing of needs for the self-sufficient cat. Owners should consult their own cat for a more complete list.

A hard lesson was that these things had to be provided, mostly on her timetable. She determined so many of my household possessions. She dictated the timing of my trips to the store, based upon her needs. She pushed me into establishing routines to her liking.

And Frodo structured my life in less obvious ways. In New York City, I was dragged by my cat-loving wife to see the same Broadway show twice—the endlessly running *Cats* by Andrew Lloyd Webber. I purchased reference books about cats and received gifts bearing cat likenesses. I considered the desirability of living in neighborhoods in rural areas with easy access to a vet's office. No flowers could be in the house because they would get tipped over. No poisonous plants like poinsettias. No floor plants because they would be dug up. And I had to pack on the sly because Frodo recognized when the luggage came out of the closet. She learned the coming change of routine.

Finally, I couldn't have photographs lying around, but that was because of Brandy. He chewed them up. Inexplicable animosity toward Eastman Kodak, I guess.

Wisdom comes from many sources. Ancient Greek political philosophers told us how life should be, while their Enlightenment counterparts explained how life really is. Scientists discover and describe the world around us. Humanists provide tools for us to get along better with one another. Religion teaches the wisdom of the prophets—that we strive to do justice, love mercy, and walk humbly.

Cats offer nothing philosophical or grand. But Frodo set an example of a simple life, well led. This sort of made her the cat equivalent of the Quakers, meant respectfully. Frodo always kept close to those she loved. She stayed near her home. She enjoyed so much the simplest pleasures and companionship of others. She suffered stoically.

Hell, she even woke up early.

For my time on this planet, I opted to contribute to the imperfect science of politics. But as the distance to the top of the ladder of life grows shorter, I am increasingly tempted to think there is much wisdom that comes with being simple and free.

8

Down East

THE SIGN GREETING AUTOMOBILE travelers as they cross the stunning Piscataqua River Bridge from Portsmouth, New Hampshire, into the Pine Tree State is "Welcome to Maine: The Way Life Should Be." This is boastful and a bit out of character for generally understated Mainers, but substantially true. Maine is an enviable combination of scenic beauty, an outdoor spirit, moderate and sensible politics, and variety that ranges from upscale Portland restaurants to Down East fishing villages. Like most outsiders moving into Maine, which is not widely known for its welcoming attitude, we were slow to learn the origin of the term "Down East." It describes the rocky coastal region of rural Maine where we were heading, named for the trade winds from the more populous areas of New England that pushed sailors to head down east to get there.

Coming down from Montreal, Canada, we crossed into Maine from the west on Route 2, near Bethel. We had quite a sampling of rural Maine as we drove the curves and valleys. Particularly notable to displaced Midwesterners was the sickeningly sweet smell of the paper mills around Rumford, Maine, where former senator Ed Muskie had grown up. The first time we encountered it, I wondered how the workers could stand it daily and how Frodo and Brandy could take the stench even temporarily with their highly sensitive sniffers. It turns out that one grows accustomed to the scent over time. Only a few miles north of the University of Maine was Old Town, a paper-mill town with the same odd smell that trickled on down to campus on heavily overcast days.

I've occasionally questioned the decision to live mostly in states with strong paper-mill or cow smells, but each state has its charms.

Smells not unlike cows sent Mom and me piling out of the Bonneville and into the light rain while temporarily parked in the lot of a motel on the Penobscot River in Bangor, Maine. We had just arrived in town on Route 2 and were taking stock of what to do next when we decided the best thing was to bail out. Frodo had picked an inopportune time to use the backseat litter box, and judging from the pungent odor, the long trip from Sioux Falls had adversely affected her digestive tract.

Once out of the car, I looked more carefully at the motel sign, which tried to attract a bevy of long-term renters by cheerily advertising its misspelled "efeiciencies" apartments. The sign stayed that way for the next ten years, much to our amusement. We later found out that the motel often served as a hostel for families coming to town to visit their loved ones at the Bangor Mental Health Institute, just up the hill.

So my first real move in my new hometown turned out to be gulping for fresh air, an inauspicious start to a new life. Following in car number two, Donna wondered why we had suddenly pulled into the parking lot of a motel and piled out into the rain. She drove up to us and rolled down her window to inquire about our next move, laughing at our misfortune after we told her. We secretly wondered if she relished the payback to those of us in the big car for those oh-so-many miles.

We decided the best course of action was to hit a restaurant and start talking to some of the locals about how to find suitable housing. From the parking lot, we could see a nearby bridge over the Penobscot River into the city of Brewer, so we headed over it. At the time, two bridges spanned the Penobscot River, connecting the towns of Bangor and Brewer. The old bridge was known by the locals as "the old bridge," while the new bridge had come to be called "the new bridge," or less often, the Chamberlain Bridge (after Joshua Chamberlain, the Civil War hero at Gettysburg, who was born in Brewer). When the state built a third bridge over the Penobscot to link the two towns, it was known initially as "the new, new bridge." As humor columnist Dave Barry often said in his heyday, I am not making this up.

"So you two are looking for a place to live, eh?" asked the waitress back to us, after we had just asked her if she had any ideas about a place to live.

"We sure are," I replied. "Do you have any ideas? We just arrived in town, and we don't have any sense of the Bangor/Brewer area. All we have is a bad map at this point. We were thinking about getting the newspaper and looking in the real-estate ads."

"Well, dearie," she counseled, "it's going to be hard to find a good place around here. The strong economy has brought new people to the area, and it's that time of year when all of the college students start coming back as well."

Sort of like when I first met Donna on the airplane, the door was opened to mention that I knew all about those college kids because I was a professor, but that seemed like too much boasting in a small

Brewer café. Instead, I mentioned a vague affiliation with the university, figuring that might help her guide us.

The waitress continued on to say that it would be difficult to find an apartment in the college town of Orono, eight miles up the road. That was okay with us; I had never lived in anywhere so small as that town of 10,000, and Donna was from the Twin Cities. (The one time we heard Bangor and Brewer referred to as the twin cities, she about doubled over in laughter.) We had decided to settle in the Bangor/Brewer area for another reason, anyway. Both of the area hospitals were located in Bangor, and Donna had to find a job to repay some of her sizable student loans. With a more regular work routine for a nurse than a professor, it made sense for me to be the one to commute.

As we were heading out the door, our waitress offered one more thought. "There are some new apartments going up in town," she said. "Head straight down Wilson Street and then turn left at Downeast Toyota. The new apartments are right behind it. Maybe you can find a place there."

We thanked her and drove straight to those apartments. We were in a hurry in order to avoid more hotels and more time with cats stuck in the car. The name of the development was Leisure Living, and the street address—Wild Rose Drive—sounded regal. These brand-new apartment buildings were adequately spaced out from one another and tastefully nestled into the pine trees. Each of the buildings held only four apartments. With a separate entrance for each unit and two floors of living space, we had plenty of privacy. No one lived above or below, only adjacent.

I had moved from a cheesy joint in Oklahoma to a swanky joint in Maine.

We loved it. The housing tip was an especially good one because we had originally planned to occupy separate quarters as we slowly built our lives together, but we instead decided to combine our assets and be roomies in this upscale place. Even my mother agreed this was the best arrangement, especially since we might quickly run out of any other housing options.

Mom had to repress a lot of years of steady churchgoing to arrive at that conclusion. Maybe the trip wore her out to the point where she took leave of her senses. But in her heart, she knew a safe place and the promise of a life together was the best thing for the two kids she was leaving behind in New England, much better than living apart in what little we could individually afford in a crowded housing market. This was especially true for Donna, who didn't have a job yet and had only scarce resources to fall back upon. We weren't sure we would find another place soon if we didn't seize this one.

Many years later, I had a funny thought about that decision to live together. I was selected as one of three finalists for the presidency of my Lutheran-affiliated alma mater, Augustana College. The selection process was bumpy, and ultimately Augustana chose the former chair of its board of trustees, while I ended up withdrawing from the search before a final decision was announced. But as part of the presidential search process, Augustana hired a firm to check out each finalist's credit history, driving record, and criminal record. I smiled to myself at the thought of passing all of the criminal tests, but getting disqualified by some top-secret tribunal because of earlier living arrangements on Wild Rose Drive.

The only catch to renting this apartment was the "no pets" provision written into the lease. We asked the amiable landlord about the possibility of cats. Anxious to fill his newly built apartments to start the cash flow, and sizing up a professor and a nurse as a pretty good risk, he said a cat would be fine. We quietly extrapolated his comment to mean one cat per person. Within a short time, he knew our secret, but he didn't say a word. We had found a home.

Our existence at Wild Rose Drive was spartan, where the word "spartan" is defined as owning much less than the Spartans owned in ancient Greece. The main piece of furniture we brought with us was that director's chair, which Brandy immediately monopolized. The rest of us were relegated to the floor because we had no beds; we had no dressers. On day two in the new apartment, Donna snapped a photo of Frodo nestled in a blanket on the floor, probably wondering why in the world we left South Dakota. This move didn't seem like upward mobility.

At least the apartment was nicely situated for the cats. We had only one neighbor on our side of the building. A small pine tree was planted right outside each front door, and a much larger one was but a few steps away. Pine trees were more fragrant than deciduous trees, and they were also good for climbing, if you were a cat, and for bird-watching. Black asphalt designed to hold parked cars provided a kitty with a warm place to lie. Best of all, an overgrown field was just a short walk away.

Within no time, Frodo embarked in search of adventure. She quickly made some new friends, the little socialite.

* * *

Madelyn was her first acquaintance. She was the elderly lady whose apartment was on the same side of the building as ours and shared the same asphalt parking lot. She owned a beautiful Oldsmobile Cutlass with virtually no miles on it because it was hardly driven. Frodo scaled the Cutlass in less than ten minutes the very first time she was outside in our new place. I envisioned claw marks on the top of the white vinyl car roof and raced over to grab her. As much as I hate to admit it, she gave me a very bitchy meow of protest, the kind the cat owner always experiences when depriving a kitty of the high ground.

Frodo of Brewer had the same go-for-the-high-ground instinct as Joshua Chamberlain of Brewer at Gettysburg; he heroically held the high ground with the 20th Maine Regiment at Little Round Top, turning the tide for the Union in that pivotal battle of the Civil War.

Madelyn obviously witnessed this scene. Even before we had been introduced to one another, she opened her door and yelled out to me, "Your little white kitty is okay. I don't mind." She was keeping tabs on the new neighbors but starting out more than reasonable.

It was only after this that I began to think of Frodo as the "little white kitty" myself, a sobriquet I use to this day.

With the little criminal in my arms, I could only mumble, "Well, thanks, but she can sit on our cars, not yours." After all, the Bonneville and Escort were broken in and nearby.

I valiantly fought but lost this battle. Maybe Frodo was signaling her desire to trade up to the low-miles Cutlass, but probably it was the better vantage point for keeping tabs on the other apartments across the way. Madelyn kept insisting it didn't matter, so eventually we just took her at face value and let Frodo of Brewer occupy the high ground. Brandy followed suit.

Lots of quality cat time was had atop the Cutlass. Oldsmobile should have thought of some of these other uses of its cars before GM executives killed the line.

Frodo soon upped the ante. She started sitting on Madelyn's outdoor step and then atop her closed-up garbage can, which sat outside her door behind that strategically planted small pine tree. Whenever I peeked out my front door, I would look toward either the car or the garbage can. My eyes would meet Frodo's, and her message was clear: *Yes, you are there and I am here. Geography is defi-*

nitely your strong suit. Now go back inside to whatever you were doing. I'm fine. She then resumed neighborhood surveillance.

Frodo upped the ante again. She parlayed her position into a game of cat and mouse, where she became the mouse. When Madelyn strolled out to retrieve her mail one day, Frodo streaked right past her through the open apartment door. It was no great feat—all of the apartments had storm doors but not screen doors, and Madelyn moved slowly.

A short time later, the telephone rang. "I think that your little white kitty just ran into my apartment," Madelyn exclaimed, "but I can't find her." Donna volunteered to troop over, figuring it was better for a woman to rummage through an elderly lady's apartment.

"Yes, you better be the one to go over and retrieve *our* cat," I concurred. "I'm quite sure Madelyn would prefer it." This was one of only a few times I recall agreeing that we shared joint custody of Frodo.

Donna eventually located Frodo on the second floor in the bedroom closet, sniffing Madelyn's clothes. She apologized profusely to Madelyn before returning to our apartment with the wannabe mouse.

"So what was the deal?" I asked. Years and years of college still handsomely paying dividends. Incisive questions every time.

"Oh, Frodo made it all the way upstairs into her bedroom and was sniffing around in her closet," replied Donna.

"Wow," I said, not wanting to top my previous words.

Frodo didn't fully appreciate the irony of being the mouse in this game of cat and mouse with Madelyn, but she loved the sport. She looked for every opportunity to squeeze past Madelyn into her apartment. She made it in probably two dozen times in the year we lived on Wild Rose Drive, which caused me to wonder whether lonely old Madelyn might be looking the other way, just a bit. Frodo was probably dumbfounded by all of the furnishings in Madelyn's place, compared to our empty nest.

We certainly did things for Madelyn to compensate for Frodo's intrusions. Donna ran to the store to fetch things and baked her blueberry muffins. I regularly retrieved Madelyn's mail, since it involved a short walk around our building to a set of apartment mailboxes. Frodo took stock of this routine and quickly learned to accompany me. After stopping at Madelyn's to pick up her mailbox key, Frodo and I took a few steps down the sidewalk, made a left-hand turn onto the asphalt parking area, another left-hand turn onto a connecting road, and a quick turn to the right to the mailboxes. Start to finish, about forty yards. As the crow flies, twenty yards. Frodo diligently trotted behind me as I made each turn, just like a—dare I say it—puppy dog.

On the return trip, though, she dispensed with the many turns and charged straight across the open grass at full speed, stopping abruptly when she hit Madelyn's sidewalk. I attributed this mad dash to life in New England. Maine was part of Massachusetts until the Missouri Compromise of 1820, and Massachusetts was the home of Paul Revere. Frodo's breathless run somehow mimicked Revere's famous cry: "The mail is coming! The mail is coming!"

Frodo returned the longer way along the asphalt path only in wintertime, when the snow made the shortcut impassable. She apparently knew the story of the Donner party crossing the Sierra Nevada.

While on the subject, Frodo was a great pal in winter. Some kitties like to romp in the snow, while others don't. She was always ready to go outside with a human. Maybe she was inspired by the example of Boomer and Sooner, the horses that pulled the Sooner Schooner onto the field when Oklahoma scored a touchdown.

The horses were four-legged, white, and spunky, just like Frodo. Or maybe the little white kitty just liked the camouflage. She could blend into snow like a chameleon.

* * *

As Frodo grew more confident about her surroundings, she ventured farther and farther into the nearby overgrown field, where she reestablished that she was the cat in search of a mouse. To reach the field, she had to angle through the shared apartment green space and pass through someone else's private backyard. The field became her favorite place. She spent countless hours over there, secretly pretending to be a lioness ready to pounce on a straggling wildebeest.

I don't think she caught many mice. In fact, she wasn't much of a hunter. Easier to catch food out of a can, she rightly figured, especially when plopped onto a plate.

Only once did Frodo deposit the proverbial dead mouse on our doorstep. Even a non-cat person knows this is customary practice for cats that snatch quarry. Their symbolic act is supposed to signal their submission and good intentions toward their human counterparts, whom they probably understand as dominant cats. But given her track record over time, I always wondered if Frodo might have found this mouse conveniently dead.

I can envision her muttering to herself, "Aw, hell, who's gonna know?"

The two-legged female of the family was, shall we say, underwhelmed with the gift. But dead was better than alive. Later on, at a different house, Frodo snatched a mouse and brought it back alive. Donna shrieked so loudly that a startled Frodo dropped the creature, which then scurried away. I laughed at both of them while Frodo stared at Donna like she had absolutely lost her marbles. I could almost hear Frodo grumble, in the voice of Eeyore the donkey, "Always figured Donna wouldn't amount to much. Said so from the start."

The overgrown field became a battleground. Frodo loved mousing so much that she often ignored my attempts to summon her. I would be in the field, calling her name. She might be only six feet away, but absolutely motionless. Thrashing about, I would stumble upon her in the high grass which would draw from her a harsh look that said, "Shhh, you're blowing it, you big-footed oaf."

One time, after we'd been there for most of a year, I was cutting through the private home's backyard en route from the field to our apartment when the man of the house popped around the corner and saw Frodo being restrained in my arms. He chuckled.

"So you own her, huh?" he asked.

"Yes, she's mine," I confessed.

"Well, my wife and I have really laughed at that cat," he said. "She comes over to our deck and stares in at us, watching us watch television. But I think she mostly comes over for the birds. I have a feeder in a few of the trees, and sometimes I see her climbing up, trying to get at the birds."

Oh no. A bird person—normally bitter enemies of cats. Moreover, this happened at the same time that some misguided representative in the Maine legislature was pushing the tired idea of making it illegal for cats to kill birds. This proposal had circulated in different states for years, an effort to force cat owners to pay compensation for protected or rare birds killed. Outlawing instinct seemed more than a little odd to cat lovers.

Here it comes, I thought to myself, *a lecture about murderous cats. And me holding the wannabe serial killer right in my arms.*

But it was nothing of the sort. He said the white kitty's hopeful efforts to scale the trees so that she might ravage the bird population were endlessly amusing. It turns out that birds fly rather than walk to birdfeeders in Maine, just like in South Dakota. No harm done.

"I'm sorry if she's been disturbing you in any way," I said. Then, struggling to restrain Frodo, who was growing bored with this conversation while resting in my arms, I apologized again.

"It's no problem," he reiterated. "She seems like a nice cat."

So Frodo and I headed off. I never learned the guy's name, and I never ran into him again because we moved away shortly after the chance encounter. But it speaks volumes about the general disposition of the little white kitty that she made friends with people whose names I never even knew.

* * *

Sure, Frodo had enemies. Territorial neighborhood kitties beat her up occasionally. She was a peacenik who followed the same losing strategy each time: arch and fluff up, turn sideways as part of a bluff that you are going to fight, then hiss and run away. Her dash for safety would only inflame their desire to wham her. And despite the mailbox wind-sprint training, she could never outrun the enemy kitties because of her mildly arthritic right rear leg.

I kept a close eye and prevented many a thrashing, but there were times that I heard the sickening wail of my gentle kitty being lacerated, usually on her hindquarters. I began thinking that her outdoor time had to be restricted. Quite a few sourpuss cats roamed the area.

Brandy provided a partial solution to the problem of the menacing neighborhood kitties. The sole survivor in the womb, he was an agile and fierce cat as he came into his own, almost the antithesis of his mother. His dominant genes came from his father, not his mother—unless, of course, I was right and he was somehow switched at birth. Either way, he actively sought out fights, and he seemed impervious to pain or infection. We always tried to stop him for the sake of his many victims, but most of the time when we heard some terrible screech, Brandy was the one beating the daylights out of some other wandering cat. His long legs allowed him to run down and topple competitors. Brandy created a safety zone outside for Frodo whenever he was outside. Even after he was neutered, he remained fiercely combative. After all, this was a cat that had carved a hole through a wire screen so he could come and go outside as he damn well pleased.

One day, we drove up to the apartment and there sat Brandy, in the dead middle of the street, as if he were taunting cars. He lost part of a front tooth that year. The vet guessed that a glancing blow by a car was the reason. The busted tooth became part of his mystique.

Despite their bad intentions, enemy kitties paled in comparison to the veterinarian on Frodo's list of despised creatures. Our apartment was close to Dr. Ladd's office at Brewer Veterinary Clinic, and he saw Frodo many times that first year in Maine for routine shots, lacerations, and flea baths. Like us, he had moved into the area recently. The first time we took Frodo to him, he noticed our Wild Rose Drive address on the paperwork—it was the same complex he had chosen to be close to work.

We had not met personally, but he recognized us. "Hey," he said to me, "you're the guy whose cat follows him to the mailbox!" I nodded, proud if slightly embarrassed.

Dr. Ladd gave Frodo excellent care, patiently explaining procedures and medications. Nurse Donna would ask about dose, drug interactions, and symptoms; I would nod stupidly, confirming the medical course of action with incisive comments like, "Okay, makes sense."

Frodo's agenda differed from ours, as we found out when she lashed out at Dr. Ladd. Both Donna and I took Frodo to the vet for her shots—Donna to ask the pertinent questions and me to comfort the patient. Maybe the office smelled like Pitocin or something and brought back bad memories. Whatever it was, Frodo did not like the feline leukemia injection one bit. When Dr. Ladd turned his back to ready another type of shot, Frodo followed him to the edge of the exam table, reached out as far as she possibly could, and took a high-velocity, claws-out swipe at him.

Take that, you sonofabitch, she thought.

She missed, but not by much. Donna and I were right there as she inched toward the edge of the table, but we didn't anticipate an actual swipe, so we didn't react in time to head it off. We couldn't quite regain our composure either, trying to explain to Dr. Ladd that with his back turned he had just narrowly escaped death at the hands of a white-furred assassin. Frodo was probably thinking that this was justifiable homicide, in self-defense.

That particular veterinary practice saved Frodo's life. On a beautiful summer Sunday, almost a year after moving to Maine, we decided to picnic at our weekend playground and future wedding site, Acadia National Park, which was exactly forty-two miles from Brewer. We let the kitties outside to romp in the morning because we planned to be gone for the day. Brandy went out and came back on schedule, apparently finding no enemy cats to rough up for sport. Frodo disappeared for hours. We waited and called, and we strolled the neighborhood looking for her. We checked everywhere, including the favorite overgrown field by the bird lover's house. Thrice I traipsed over there.

Our initial amusement at her stealth gave way to impatience, then to concern. She was missing far too long.

In a remark she later regretted, Donna suggested that we just leave Frodo outside and come back early. *What?* I thought. *Violate my established and announced principle of not leaving the house for a long time with a kitty outside? No, I don't think so.* At that precise moment, I agreed with Frodo's earliest assessment that Donna wouldn't amount to much after all.

We ate a very late picnic lunch on the floor of our apartment, completely abandoning our trip to Acadia. In late afternoon, many hours after she had gone out, Frodo slowly trudged up the sidewalk to the door.

Her tail literally dragged behind her.

We never found out how or why, but Frodo was drenched in motor oil. A black layer hid much of her white fur, especially around her hindquarters. She couldn't hold up her tail due to the weight of the oil. I certainly hope it was some weird accident, as innocent as her getting into mischief at nearby Downeast Toyota.

Donna and I panicked. We rushed her upstairs and wrapped her in a bathroom towel to absorb the oil. We filled the tub with lukewarm water with the idea of scrubbing her fur. Frodo's eyes seemed glossed over, maybe from fatigue, but we worried she might have ingested oil in an effort to clean herself. The vet's office was closed on Sunday, but they quickly returned our emergency call. They advised a long series of baths, promising to take her if we needed their help. Thinking minutes might be critical to her survival, we probably started scrubbing too vigorously. Frodo panicked. She climbed my back, lacerating the skin as I bent over the tub.

She was out of control. Soap only seemed to worsen the problem by congealing the oil. We called the vet back and said we were on our way. I held Frodo in a tightly wrapped towel as we drove. She was messy, weary, and terrified.

A cat covered head-to-toe in motor oil. And I thought a cesarean section an unlikely event.

We were grateful the vet's office was nearby. A vet tech greeted us in the parking lot, having arrived simultaneously. She opened up the office while listening briefly to the story. She swiftly called for more assistance and then marched to the back room with Frodo still wrapped in the towel, probably to sedate her. She said that she would call us when she knew something more, reminiscent of the sequence of events involving Frodo's cesarean section.

We paced the apartment for about two hours, waiting for the telephone to ring. We worried about her coat, eyes, and skin. We also worried about her life, not knowing if she had ingested oil, or how much was fatal. Was she strong enough to endure treatment?

Finally, the telephone rang. We planned all along for Donna to take the call, thinking it best that the nurse hear the medical report. Donna listened intently for what seemed like an eternity to me. At last, she broke into outright laughter. "Okay," she said, "we'll be there tomorrow morning to pick her up." Then she hung up.

I was reassured but slightly put off by the laughter and exceedingly curious about the other end of the phone conversation.

"What happened?" I asked anxiously. "How's my Frodo? Is she okay?"

"Yeah, she's okay," Donna replied drily. She seemed to be holding back good news just a little bit longer than decency allowed. "They did have to sedate her because she was going a little crazy, and they had to give her multiple baths to get the oil out of her fur. She can't come home until tomorrow, but they don't think she ingested any of the motor oil, and she seems to be recovering just fine."

"So then what was so funny?" I asked indignantly.

"Well, regular soap and water didn't seem to work any better for them than it did for us, so they switched over to Tide. Yeah, they cleaned up your little white kitty princess with laundry detergent. It took four washings."

Four wash and rinse cycles for my precious kitty? The only consolation in this twisted set of events was that the vet's office was filled with good people, so I knew they had operated with their most delicate cycle.

The bill from the vet the next day itemized the charges, mostly related to the emergency visit and the overnight stay. But one line near the bottom of the bill for Frodo Moen read "4 baths, $20."

After that goofy incident, Dr. Ladd always chuckled whenever he saw the white kitty with me outside. He wasn't personally involved with the Tide baths, but the story had obviously circulated throughout the office.

And I can only imagine what was written down in Frodo Moen's chart. Something along these lines, I suppose: "Owner reports his cat must have accidentally fallen into vat of motor oil. Owner lacks additional info about trauma. Note to file—owner may be a nutcase."

When we retrieved Frodo from the vet, she was as white as a sheet and as fragrant as a flower. She seemed downright tickled at her own elegance. She stayed inside for the rest of the day and the next morning to recuperate, but in the afternoon she strolled out and promptly dropped on the warm asphalt, straight in the dirt, as always. Yet the great oil incident would change how we approached her outdoor time, and not to her liking.

* * *

While Frodo gradually expanded her network of friends over the course of that first year in Maine, I remained at the center. Donna did everything possible for Frodo because she loved all kitty cats, but Frodo would routinely walk right over her on the couch to get to me. If I came into a room and sat down, Frodo jumped off Donna (or anyone else, for that matter) and headed straight for my lap. And when I used to click my thumb and forefinger together and plead for her to come over, she usually walked straight over. She never lost the belief that we were together. Her unswerving affection sometimes drove cat-loving Donna crazy, but she slowly accepted and eventually respected Frodo's fierce loyalty. She concomitantly grew close to Brandy, who warmed up to her and eventually only to her.

Frodo was my constant companion that year. I worked days at the university, while Donna worked nights and weekends at Eastern Maine Medical Center, so we saw little of each other. Frodo was a steady friend in this new place. She provided endless calm during a stressful time that included moving, an intensified relationship with a woman, and a newly launched career. She cushioned my loneliness for my parents, now living halfway across the North American continent. She often sat quietly in my arms or slept motionless on my legs, which she loved because they were suitably long. At those times, we provided one another an easy, peaceful station in life.

9

Diverging Paths

OUR PROFESSIONAL LIVES SOON
gained traction. The University of Maine proved to be a terrific
place to launch an academic career. Students piled into the political
science courses I taught and provided high course evaluations.
The University of Alabama Press published my first scholarly book
and asked for rights to a second; refereed journal articles found
their way into print and so did an edited volume with Temple
University Press. Ed was a terrific department chairperson, and
Ken started incorporating me into state government and Maine
politics research. Donna switched to much better hours at Eastern
Maine Medical Center, where she became the charge nurse on the
labor and delivery floor.

On the home front, though, things were tougher. The two kitties
got us booted from our wonderful apartment at Leisure Living on
Wild Rose Drive. The one-kitty-each rule we successfully pioneered
at the apartment complex led to the establishment of a regional cattery
in the landlord's mind, and he was all done with it. As the first wave of

new tenants left the complex after their one-year leases were up, the landlord found oodles of fleas in his brand-new apartments. He sent every tenant a copy of the "no pets" clause, along with a deadline for eviction. I called him, thinking we might be grandfathered in because we were among the first to bring cats into the complex.

I misjudged. He was well aware that we abetted the problem of cats proliferating like bunnies. We could get rid of the cats, he said, or we could move out—our choice. It was not too much of a decision. By then, I'd been with Frodo through a cesarean section, raising a kitten, far-flung travel, different homes, scuffles with other cats, fleas and shots, and an oil dip and four Tide baths. I loved her. Tossing her in order to stay in an apartment wasn't really an option, so we started apartment shopping. Donna found us a place quickly, and we moved out well before eviction.

I'm not sure I ever told Mom about actually being evicted from the apartment, for fear of garnering a "dumb bunny" designation.

Moving was still pretty easy because we hadn't accumulated a whole lot, but we had moved up in the world a little bit. We now owned a couple of cheap dressers purchased at the Brewer used-furniture place located at the base of the new bridge, sandwiched between the old bridge and the future location of the new, new bridge. The crusty Mainer who sold us the dressers also sold antiques and just about anything else, but his principal occupation was less salesman than political commentator. Like so many Mainers, he knew instantly that we weren't from the area because we pronounced the final consonant with words ending in the letter *r* and we didn't add an *r* to words ending in a vowel, as they often do in New England.

Donna's name, for instance, was pronounced by area Mainers as "Donner," like the reindeer.

After selling us the merchandise and confirming that we were "from away"—the term used by Mainers to describe the not-always-welcome interlopers to The Way Life Should Be— he started telling us that Maine was a splendid place to live because it lacked any real racial diversity. Everyone was white, he said. This wannabe Klansman probably relished the idea of a little white kitty.

He offered additional tips on incorporating into Maine culture, then freely dispensed advice about personal relationships. Oh joy.

Along with the dressers, we now owned a bed, a plaid couch and matching chair, and a kitchen table with four chairs. The only possession we chose to leave behind in our move out of Leisure Living was our three-story cat condominium. It was built in the spirit of love for our two kitties, mostly out of plywood and carpet remnants picked up at Marden's, a fire-sale liquidation store of sorts whose ditty was "I should have bought it / when I saw it / at Marden's." But the kitty condo had a fatal flaw.

An architect or engineer would describe the building flaw this way: too tall, not wide enough. Yeah, the political scientist and the nurse teamed up to build a structure that was, uh, too tall, not wide enough. Never mind that we accidentally cut into our first kitchen table in the building process, by using it as a sawhorse.

The kitties of Brewer really only liked story three, of course, and they always leapt upward from the big-box television set to the top of the defective kitty condo. For the next eight seconds, they rode out the ensuing motion like a Hawaiian surfer, until pure physics stopped the condo from swaying.

While in woodworking class in junior high, I had massacred both the birdhouse and the chessboard project. These substandard carpentry skills combined with a flawed design to create one sorry-ass cat condo. Luckily, our next major construction project corrected all of our mistakes.

Our new surroundings were less desirable in every way, except for the fact that we moved up from one bedroom to two. Our official address was Eastern Avenue, still in Brewer, and right across the street from the high-school football field. On fall weekends, we took in the noise of the Brewer Witches fans. (After we lived in Maine for a while, we discovered that there were quite a few dyed-in-the-wool, self-proclaimed witches living in the remote woods of the Pine Tree State.) Our back deck looked right into a tall wooden fence intended to separate apartment dwellers from homeowners. It was reminiscent of the big concrete wall that Frodo and I stared at out our front door at Ashley Square in Norman. Our new apartment was poorly insulated and like an icicle in the winter, with expensive New England electric heat to boot, so we did as the rest of the tenants and blow-dried hot plastic over all of our windows to cut down on drafts. There is nothing more gratifying than living all winter long without seeing out a window in order to save a dollar. The cats thought the plastic absolutely sucked. We tussled with them many times over pristine versus shredded plastic. Brandy—aka screen boy—was a special problem.

At Leisure Living, Madelyn never made a peep that we heard, and our country-style life was serene. At our new place, which was more of an in-town condominium, we shared a common wall both upstairs and downstairs with a set of neighbors. The walls might as well have been nonexistent, they were so thin, and Lisa and Doug were passionate people. Passionate in their disagreements too, and we heard almost every word exchanged between our neighbors over the next year. A particularly memorable exchange was Lisa shouting out in anger, "Doug, you act like I'm an ugly old bag!"

Doug's acid reply? "Well, you're old." She was probably thirty-two at the time.

The kitties never appreciated how we decreased the quality of our lifestyle to get into a place that allowed pets. As I've said before, gratitude is not a strong suit of cats.

* * *

Frodo could see no reason to move, but she adjusted to the new apartment. She liked the additional space, which meant a more privately situated litter box. This was an especially helpful development since her truant son had taken to pouncing on her for sport as she came out of the litter box. Not every time, but on occasion.

Brandy continued struggling with his dominant/submissive cat complex. You could see it in his behavior. Part of his outlook was, "Hey mom, I'm taller, bigger, faster, meaner, smarter, and more alert than you." Proof of this was the time he took a spin in the stackable dryer at Leisure Living, after jumping atop the warm clothes when Donna turned her back with the dryer door open. He spun but a time or two before Donna heard the massive thud of a twelve-pound cat surfing aimlessly with the towels. She released him, fluffed slightly but not any cleaner since he hadn't received a Tide bath first. Although he no doubt felt rather discombobulated, he seemed defiant and still quite proud, with his probably bruised head held high as he came out.

Counterbalancing the dominant-cat sentiment were the times he leapt onto the couch to be next to his mom. He loved to lie down beside her, but he could so easily get smacked in the process. He used to jump up next to Frodo and then absolutely freeze. Motionless he would remain for up to ten seconds. A suitable time having elapsed, he would slowly and successfully lie down by her, but only back-to-back. When pouncing on his mom for fun, he was dominant, but lying beside her he was absolutely subservient.

Poor Brandy. Manly like Arnold Schwarzenegger, but with something like an Oedipus complex.

For the cats, the new apartment's best feature was the dining room. In fact, any real-estate booklet describing the apartment would have said of the dining room, in the interests of full disclosure, "Dining room designed by a kitty, for a kitty." It had an open ledge connecting to the kitchen, intended to give human occupants a way to see into the dining room, or perhaps a place to set small plants or household collectibles. But to a cat, the ledge was just a part of a multistep going-up-higher process, easily summarized this way: floor to chair (leap), chair to table (leap), table to open ledge (leap), eyes/nose focused on kitchen stove/sink/countertops (stare/sniff).

We discouraged it. We kept the chairs tucked under the table, but the cats just skipped the first step and leapt straight atop the table. We crowded the ledge with several items, but they jumped with flare and bravado anyway, and without much thought to collateral damage. When something flew off after they landed on the ledge, they would peer from their perch over the side at it. One of those surprised cat looks followed, where ears are standing straight up and eyes are focused intently to determine if the inanimate object that just shattered into a thousand pieces might still wiggle.

Damn, they would say to themselves, *just another dead flower vase.*

We yelled at them. "Brandyyy!" was a common cry. And just like a mom yelling the full name or the full and middle name of a kid when she's really angry, we reinserted the vowel for the white princess and hollered, "Frodooo!"

The ledge was the basis for the only time that I ever heard my aunt Clara Marie swear. She and my aunt Margie came from South Dakota to Maine for our wedding in the beautiful Asticou Garden on the coast at Northeast Harbor. Typical aunts, they did a couple million things that went unappreciated, but one that was noticed was their cooking for the tribe of twenty or so that also journeyed from the Midwest to attend our small wedding. With everyone headquartered in the Brewer Motor Inn, on the other side of the football field of the Brewer Witches, our apartment became the hangout place for quite a few days in advance of our wedding. Everyone arrived early for a mini-vacation in the place where we lived life the way it should be.

Frodo loved monitoring the kitchen labors of the two aunts, like a Roman centurion tasked with overseeing the work of gypsy slaves. The ledge was the perfect perch to do so, sort of like standing atop Cadillac Mountain in Acadia National Park near Maine's Bar Harbor, the first spot in the continental United States where the sun hits each morning. The aunts knew that I dearly loved Frodo, and they struggled mightily to ignore her participant observation, but a cat on a kitchen countertop was a bit too much for a couple of farm girls from the Midwest.

I was barely within earshot, walking slowly toward the kitchen from the living room, when Aunt Margie asked Aunt Clara Marie, "So how's dinner coming?"

The terse reply I overheard? "Fine, except for the *damn* cat."

Following her inflammatory comment, Aunt Clara Marie plucked Frodo off the ledge and gently set her down on the kitchen floor. The white kitty vocally protested this treatment; it was inconsistent with general household practice and at odds with Frodo's understanding of her natural rights. As for me, upon hearing "the damn cat," I quietly backpedaled away from the kitchen and tiptoed back into the living room, not wanting to sell out Frodo but not wanting to cook either. It was not one of my proudest moments.

The only good news was the realization that oafs can sneak out on aunts.

* * *

By the time the aunts visited, my professional career and Donna's were rolling right along, and we were starting to save money for a down payment on a house. We didn't know where we would be living in the area, but we were sure it wouldn't be anywhere close to our noisy next-apartment-over neighbors.

Frodo, on the other hand, was bored silly by the time the aunts visited. Our fortunes had truly diverged. For about the last year, she had been a fully indoor cat. The saddest time of her life, I think. She craved the feel of the earth beneath her paws and the smells of the great outdoors. It greatly saddened us, because we knew how she longed to be free. All her life, she had been an outdoor cat. Every day, she begged us to go out. Our rejection crushed her each time, as though it were the first.

Why did we do it? Outdoors at the first apartment led to lacerations, fleas, one dead mouse, and the life-threatening oil incident. This new in-town place had busy streets, dogs, and quite a few small children and teens. A stouthearted and wily fellow like Brandy could make it, but not the trusting white princess. She would get hurt or kidnapped. Unfortunately for Brandy, one cat in meant two cats in. But he accepted the change better than she did.

Frodo remained very loving, but she was dispirited. She ate out of boredom, leading to unhealthy weight gain and the beginning of digestive problems. She sat in open windows in the nice weather, when the plastic was off, sniffing the gentle breezes and assimilating what she could of the world beyond our walls. She gazed at birds and did the kitty stutter to them—the peeling back of the kitty lips and a vague sort of smiling, along with the indecipherable chattering that translated into English is something like, "Here, birdie birdie. Come play." This universal weird cat speech is something akin to Tolkien's ancient languages, like Elfish. Maybe Frodo was recalling her days of freedom, or the friends whose names I did not know. What I did know was that her sad eyes affected me. I promised to myself to compensate her for this lost time, even if I had to sacrifice a little bit to do it. My sacrifice would be time spent outdoors supervising her at new places and taking a tumble in order to protect her.

* * *

Not everything was glum. Frodo enjoyed locating the most comfortable spot in the apartment, which meant trying out many different places. Her favorite piece of furniture was me. Taking an anthropological cue from her wild ancestors, who patted down wild grasses by spinning around in a circle before plopping down, Frodo walked in a circle to pat down my lap before she dropped down. Then she stretched up for a rubby before dozing off. She lay there as long as I would endure it. When she jumped up onto a chair or couch and found my legs crossed, Frodo would look up at me with the "hey, we've got a routine here" look on her face. She didn't care that lap sleeping was more comfortable for the sleeper than the sleepee.

Donna's femur was irritatingly short and her thighs irritatingly narrow. Frodo would jump up and pat down Donna's lap, but way too much wriggling was required, and it wasn't very comfortable. Typically, it didn't work out at all, which is why she was always willing to move onto me when I arrived on the scene. Frodo would look wistfully at Donna, as if to say, "So, this is the best you've got, right? You can't fix this? You can't get, like, longer legs, or maybe a bigger backside and fatter thighs?"

For the record, I'm not sure it is wise to reference my wife's backside in a book, but at least the book isn't indexed, so the category "wife" followed by the subcategory "backside, size of" doesn't appear in print at the back.

We tried hard to perk up Frodo in her dark days indoors. We occasionally took her along for a ride in the car to see new sights and hear new sounds, just frequently enough that she did not dread automobile travel quite so much. One time, as we were heading out of town we drove through some pine trees close to the road. Frodo took full advantage by breathing deeply through a cracked window, then sticking her paw through it as though her fattened-up little body was going to squeeze through a window open only a fraction of her size. But somehow that simple act had its desired effect upon Donna and me. We realized that she needed to be a free kitty cat; we had to buy a house soon, somewhere in Maine's twin cities where she would again be allowed to roam. Our interests all coincided.

Things had gone totally awry in the apartment anyway. We had a flea infestation. A creepy and overwhelming flea infestation. The culprits were probably the stray cats and the less-cared-for kitties that roamed the apartment complex, depositing fleas in the thick green grasses next to the doors of the individual apartments.

We knew what the two kitties were thinking—it was well past time to move. No self-respecting cats stay in places where somebody else gives 'em fleas.

Whatever the source, our last summer at the apartment had hatched many fleas. Conditions were just right for them to proliferate, and they were everywhere. We returned from a day at Acadia National Park, where we used to go hiking almost every weekend, to find a maintenance guy fumbling with the key to our apartment.

"Problem of some kind?" I asked politely as we came up behind him.

"Well, I can't make this key work, and I need to get back inside to check on the flea bombs," he replied.

"To check on *what*?" I asked sharply.

"The flea bombs. I bombed your apartment and need to check on the results," he said in a matter-of-fact tone.

I responded to him with some non-Lutheran words that my mom knows I know but deep down hopes I never really use. I expected to find Frodo and Brandy asphyxiated or at least wheezing under the bed. Instead, they sat idly by the door. They had just awoken and had stumbled to the door to meet us, having heard the endless bumbling with the key.

"Oh, this isn't the one I bombed," said the maintenance man, once the apartment was opened. I sheepishly mumbled some Lutheran rhetoric about forgiveness, rhetoric that both my mom and my wife think I should use more often.

Even things done with love started to not work out at the apartment. Fleas gave Frodo and Brandy their only known case of intestinal worms. I tried resolving this common malady with an over-the-counter cat medicine from a local supermarket. Already the veterinarians were likely driving fancy automobiles because of us; I did not want to buy them sports cars too.

I gave a full dose to each cat, secretly lacing their moist cat food, much like the conspirator in the royal court of the Middle Ages, but toward a good end. Liver flavor, their favorite. I set the food down on the floor, watched them both start eating, and walked away from a job well done.

Frodo had a slight tic as she lay on my lap that night. Every twenty seconds or so, her head just sort of bobbed. At first, I thought it was my imagination. But as it kept up, I finally called nurse Donna, who was working the evening shift at Eastern Maine Medical Center, where years later our daughter Erika would be born. My sincere hope was that Donna could somehow put the delivering women on hold while the two of us talked over the possibility of a bobbing cat head.

"Well, why don't you just watch her closely?" an exasperated Donna asked. I could tell that she thought this overprotective thing had gone a little too far this time.

Well, duh, I secretly thought. *That's what I've been doing.* But being a smart husband, I replied with something more along these lines: "Gee, that's really great advice, honey. Sure, I'll keep watching her closely and get back to you if the situation changes."

Well, the situation didn't change. So there I sat, alone with the cat for the evening in the apartment, with the charge nurse stuck at work and unlikely to run out on the nurses or the delivering patients to gauge the extent of the head bobbing.

Some medical professional, I harrumphed as the clock ticked. All she had given me was some kind of wait-and-see, lackadaisical, HMO-managed-care, go-ahead-and-wait-for-certain-death response for my beloved Frodo.

Convinced this was becoming something major, I called our friendly veterinarian, Dr. Ladd. I slightly exaggerated Frodo's symptoms to boost the chances he would agree to see her yet again after hours. "Yes, her head is *constantly* bobbing," I said, "and she just doesn't look or act right."

"Okay, bring her over," Dr. Ladd said. He must have been amused by the sheer idiocy of the problems we brought to his attention. Somewhere he's probably writing his own book about the top 100 stupid cat owners he has ever known, with me contending for the top spot.

I hung up the phone and ran over to Brewer Vet with the princess.

Upon arrival, I reiterated the symptoms. He checked her vital signs. He looked at her long and hard to discern whether there really was a tic. Finally, he decided in the affirmative.

"Well," he said, "she looks and acts fine except for the tic. Could she have gotten into something?"

Oh, double bananas. *Hello, Matt.* I paused momentarily before replying, weighing my beloved kitty's health against complete and total personal humiliation. Think more highly of me now than you have been, because Frodo won out. I owned up to my mistake.

"Well, I did give her and Brandy some over-the-counter worm medicine earlier."

"Any chance you overdosed her?" Dr. Ladd asked. "She shows some signs."

My heart sank. "Well, if so, certainly not on purpose," I replied defensively, stating the obvious. "But come to think of it, she could have eaten Brandy's food and accidentally received a double dose." Although I had watched them start to eat, I had left the room before they finished.

So now the situation was clear. Frodo's stomach was responsible for Frodo's bobbing head. Dr. Ladd asked about the specific brand of medicine, and he disappeared into his back office while I stared at the white kitty bobblehead in front of me.

He reemerged with a book on prescription drugs.

"I think everything will be okay," he announced after studying the book for several minutes. "Her body is metabolizing the excess. You can leave her here overnight if you wish for observation, but I think the best thing would be to take her home. No doubt you'll watch her closer than anyone."

Yeah, no doubt.

Boy, did I ever feel ridiculous. This topped the time I fell off the truck while working at P&M Steel Company for my dad in the summers, and it even beat the occasion that I cut 400 rebars (to set in concrete) six inches too short. Those qualified as dumb-bunny episodes.

At least my mistakes were less embarrassing than the mistake of the young guy who called into the women's health clinic where

Donna once worked. He earnestly reported his girlfriend sick, and he asked Donna whether he should go ahead and take his sick girlfriend's birth control pills for the time being, in order to stave off pregnancy. Apparently it didn't occur to him to take a respite until she felt better. He was motivated more like a real bunny than a dumb bunny.

Despite Dr. Ladd's reassurance that these things do happen in our attempts to do the right thing, he must have thought me a fool with a capital *F*. Like the time I dropped Frodo off after hours of unproductive labor, I slunk out of the veterinarian's office.

In a fitting end to the dark days of worm medicine poisoning, pesky fleas imported by stray cats and humans, endless months without windows to the world and access to the great outdoors, Frodo broke the very tip of her tail jumping off the stacked U-Haul boxes for the move. We took her to the vet, but there was nothing to do but let it heal. Only careful observers would ever notice the tip of her tail pointing slightly off-kilter in the years ahead.

10

The Skylight Caper

JoAnn and Don were the wife-and-husband real-estate team that worked with us to buy a house in Bangor. Bangor put us on the right side of the Penobscot River for our places of employment. After three years in Maine, we had come to like Bangor. Most people probably think of it as way up in the forests of Down East, but it had a quaint downtown, a number of good restaurants that served locals and tourists, an airport and a nice mall, good hospitals, a links-style municipal golf course, and a famous local citizen, the horror writer Stephen King. The wonderfully wild Penobscot River and the Kenduskeag Stream flowed out of the Maine mountains and melded together in downtown Bangor, thus requiring the aforementioned old bridge, new bridge, and new, new bridge.

JoAnn kept referring to the structure on Pearl Street as a dollhouse. Refurbished from top to bottom expressly for resale, this itsy-bitsy, teeny-tiny, one-and-one-half-story house's signature feature was two mirrored skylights embedded in a sloped ceiling in a beautifully restored pine living room. The rest of the house wasn't much, but at a sale price in the $60,000s, one can't ask for much more than an apartment-like house with two skylights.

We didn't think that much about it when we walked through the house, but once we moved in, the term "dollhouse" took on new meaning. Barbie (Donna) fit in the dollhouse, but Ken (Matt) did not. Particular choke points were the six-foot-high doorways at two locations, with Ken coming in at six feet, two inches tall. One of these was the sole house bathroom, which was grafted onto the first floor at the back of the house and propped up underneath with a set of jacks. After living for a couple of years on Pearl Street, we noticed the bathroom ever so slowly separating from the rest of the house. We hired a contractor to close the gap by propping the bathroom back up with timbers firmly set underneath. The other option was to be relaxing in the tub someday and start rolling down into the backyard as the structure gave way. Even the normally non-gossipy Mainers would have talked that one up, especially since it would have involved a couple of those imported types from the Midwest.

The other choke point was our bedroom door, which was a tight fit after steep stairs and a sharp corner. Not occurring to us at all until we actually moved in was that the corner was so tight we could not move our queen-size box spring into our bedroom. We pulled out a saw and made a few selective cuts, trying to get just enough bend-ability to get it around the corner, with the thought of reinforcing the frame once we housed it in the bedroom. But my carpentry skills being what they were from middle school forward, all we managed to do was mangle the frame, making it unusable without ever actually getting the bed in the room. We finally opted for a water bed, which we could get up the steps easily. That worked nicely, although we lived in fear that the extremely heavy water bed might someday crash right through the floor of the dollhouse, right on top of the kitchen, setting off a chain reaction that caused an already dangling bathroom to slide into the backyard. We experienced a big adrenaline rush at bedtime that first night, wondering if the extra weight of two human bodies and two cat bodies might be enough to tip the balance.

Frodo had thickened up as an indoor cat, adding to the precariousness of it all. The skinny wife was the offset. And maybe it helped that Brandy had lost part of his front tooth to that car.

In the wee hours of the night, heading out to use the bathroom meant that I needed to get past the slanted ceiling in our bedroom (duck), out the bedroom door (duck two inches), around the tight corner (tilt), down the steep stairs (hold on), across the cold linoleum floor (brrr), and through the bathroom door (duck again, two inches).

The pathway to the destination made me feel like the great explorer Marco Polo.

One virtue of the house was an unfinished basement, which the contractor who refurbished the house had used as a workshop. A funny aspect was the pegboard he had hung his tools on. What was funny was not the pegboard itself but rather the fact that he had traced all of his individual tools on the pegboard with a heavy black marker, so one could see exactly what shaped tool was supposed to go where. I may have suffered from FOCD—Frodo obsessive-compulsive disorder—but at least my disorder involved gentle care of a living creature, not tirelessly organizing my screwdrivers and hammers by shape.

We used the unfinished basement to construct the queen mother of all kitty condos, learning from experience and rectifying our previous errors. Since the height-to-width ratio was off on condo number one, for condo number two we used two-by-fours with two-and-a-half-inch wood screws in a triangular design that molded perfectly into the lower part of our sloped ceiling in the pine room, providing added balance and support. We wrapped a rope around a set of those two-by-fours for scratching purposes, and by tying it all together, added yet another safety feature.

Any random house inspector would have immediately realized that the condo would be standing long after the water bed had crushed the kitchen and the bathroom had fallen into the backyard.

The kitties loved it! As it was built solidly enough to outlast the pyramids, the kitties felt very comfortable with this structure. No more Hawaiian surfing when they jumped on it.

Both kitties would head to the top level. If Frodo happened to be there when Brandy showed up, he would play dominant cat and push her off to the lower level. Floor three put that fierce boy right at eye level when you walked over to him, and believe me, one thought twice about making a wrong move. He loved us, but he was capable of removing desirable anatomical human features, like faces and hands.

Both kitties especially loved the carpeted ramp, which doubled as an exquisite cat scratching post and escalator to the upper levels. They clawed and walked on it endlessly— up and down, up and down.

Our kitty cats never harmed the furniture or carpet in the doll-house. They readily adopted cat condo number two for all of their clawing needs.

* * *

Oh my god, the sheer joy when Frodo stepped outside on her own for the first time in more than a year. I let her out on the small back deck of our new house and watched her gulp in the crisp air of winter. A liberated woman, such a twinkle in the eye! The words of the old religious spiritual made so famous by the Reverend Martin Luther King Jr. fit the moment: "Free at last! Free at last! Thank God Almighty ... free at last!"

As a matter of fact, our house was a sieve in terms of keeping cats indoors. Too many ways to freedom existed. Front door. Side door. Deck door. Cellar door too, protruding up from the ground and pitched away from the house so that a person could climb straight up the stairs from the unfinished basement into the backyard. On occasion, a basement window was also an avenue of escape since we didn't own screens to fit those windows. Unfortunate that there were no black-marker outlines of window screens on the basement pegboard or we might have owned them.

Five total avenues of escape.

Frodo and Brandy acted like cops on Main Street in a small town, or maybe a little bit like Barney Fife on *The Andy Griffith Show*, strolling around the premises looking for any unlocked or open doors. But whereas Barney always worried about someone breaking into a residence in Mayberry to burgle it, our two plotted to break out like convicts in the joint at Alcatraz.

The kitty condo was their shared lookout tower. From that perch, a cat could observe all three doors—front, side, and deck. The cats could easily hear or see people approaching. Through body language and actions, the cats signaled one another: "Open door! Open door! *Run for it!*" Both cats sprinted to squeeze out—especially at first, since they were making up for lost time.

A favorite destination was Bud's house across the street. Our immediate neighbors on one side had an impenetrable chain link fence, so they were boring and inaccessible. On the other side of us lived an utterly mellow cat named Banjo—a beautiful, big-eyed, long-haired Himalayan that our neighbors had found abandoned at a lake.

Donna and I loved Banjo to pieces. He was a gigantic marshmallow. But our cats had a different opinion of him, and their attitude toward him was completely unlike their relationship with any other cat they ever encountered. Frodo and Brandy sized up Banjo as a total loser, not worth a bucket of warm spit, as the job of vice president of the United States was once described. Our cats didn't care if he was on our property. They didn't care if he was on our deck. They didn't care if he was sitting in our house upon our furniture. He wasn't worth a nod, let alone a fight, even for Brandy, who constantly sought out a good scrap. Our cats utterly ignored him.

Banjo was the Dalai Lama of the cat world, bringing peace to all who met him.

Our kitties loved to cross the street to Bud's house, and Banjo would follow, walking a few steps behind. Both of our kitties looked like they were just trying to ditch him, to vote him off their island. Banjo was the slide-rule, pocket-protector, very-thick-glasses kind of guy in cat world, compared to our two kitties, the homecoming queen and quarterback. Frodo was easier (and even Banjo sensed less risky) to tail than Brandy, so most of the time Banjo waddled across Pearl Street behind her. She glanced back as she made her way toward Bud's front steps, shooting him looks that said, "Get out of here. Get away. Get a job. Get a life." Banjo sometimes sat down in the road until the glance abated and Frodo restarted her brief sojourn to see Bud. Then he stood back up and again waddled after her.

Never did two cats pay less attention to a rival cat than ours did to Banjo.

Bud's place was kitty heaven. Planters mounted on his front windows were within an easy leap from the front steps. Frodo jumped up on them constantly so she could stare right through the windows into his living room. A little voyeur, she had also peeked into the windows of the residents by Wild Rose Drive. *Drat the lack of teeny-tiny cat opera glasses,* she probably thought.

Bud grew everything green that could survive the Maine winters, so a stroll through his yard was like touring the National Arboretum in Washington, DC.

There was an abundance of good sniffs for a cat. Bud had a large and well-positioned deck for sunning, a quiet manner, a leisurely pace because of retirement, and occasional cat treats. Frodo liked having a second home, especially one within easy walking distance. She just had to ditch Banjo the bozo.

Our property was also cat friendly. Absolutely outstanding trees rose high above the house, perfectly positioned on the lot. A favorite tree hung over the roof above the pine living room with the mirrored skylights. Perhaps you sense where this story is heading.

Donna experienced it first. She was reclining in an easy chair, reading a book by the light of day while I was downstairs, no doubt inventorying which tools I should buy at the store to fill the pegboard tracings. The sun was shining brightly through the skylights and dispersing beautifully and evenly throughout the room because of the built-in four-way mirrors.

Donna glanced up from her book.

And what to Donner's wondrous eyes should appear?

No, not little reindeer. Frodo was staring straight down at her through the skylight. Actually, dozens and dozens of Frodos were staring straight at her because of the multiple reflections emanating from the quadrangular mirror.

"Hey, Matt," Donna yelled, "*your* cat is on the roof, staring down at me."

I came bounding up the stairs. "What did you say?"

"I said your cat is on the roof, staring at me. See for yourself." She pointed up.

Frodo was now looking straight down at me too. Well, dozens and dozens of Frodos, all with the same "this is cool" look on their faces. Frodo of Brewer had once again captured the high ground.

Sometimes husbands mess up. This was one of those times.

"How did Frodo get up there?" I asked.

It was a reasonable question, since I knew she couldn't jump up, nor had she been beamed up like Scotty on *Star Trek*. Donna just shrugged. That wasn't the question that resulted in trouble. Here was the one that did: "How did she get up there when you were supposed to be watching her?"

That question was edgier and vastly more accusatory. As wives sometimes do, she replied factually but acidly, without so much as raising her voice. She pointed out to me that this happened on my watch too, was really the cat's doing, and involved my precious little white princess.

She said "princess" sort of sarcastically. Suddenly, I felt like Banjo the bozo.

"Well, it really doesn't matter who's at fault here," I responded. "The important thing is that we get her down safely and figure out a way to stop it from happening again."

Smooth backpedal, I thought smugly to myself. *Way to go.*

It turns out that Frodo shimmied up the pine tree growing alongside the house and leapt from it onto the roof. Having blazed a path, she started doing it almost every time she went outside. I've often thought that in the summer months, she lived the concept of Cat on a Hot Tin Roof.

Since the tree branches were higher than the roof, Frodo would not reverse direction. Each time, I had to rescue her. Otherwise, she would just stay up there yowling about the unfairness of being stranded atop a small roof and the importance of being set back down on earth immediately. Most effective was a stepladder that I left sitting on the deck in perpetuity expressly for this purpose, though I was never especially fond of ladders. Heights appealed more to my kitty cats than to me.

At least in theory, a quicker way that completely avoided ladders was standing on the slanted cellar door, holding the roof with one hand and the cat in the other, and then stepping back gingerly off the cellar door. This was generally an easy and fairly risk-free method, at least in summer. The only difficult dilemma was Frodo stopping short on the roof, just barely out of arm's reach. I usually extended my fingers for a rubby and then made a quick grab. Often, I would have to do this several times before I was able to nab and thereby rescue her.

A second drawback of the cellar-door method was the slight risk of an accident, especially in inclement weather. One winter day, both Donna and I were outside scooping snow from the driveway in front of the house. Frodo was outside with us, fluffing the snow, as she was prone to do, when she started her customary wild dash to gain momentum for going up the tree. Up she went. At the point of the actual jump from tree to roof, she typically paused and gathered her balance and strength. She leapt on over, landing with a soft thud and a couple more cat scratches in the asphalt shingles as she dug in. On this day, she explored while we scooped. Then the meowing to get down began.

All summer and fall, I had practiced the standing-on-the-cellar-door-and-hanging-on-to-the-roof removal method. Yeah, I was a professional. So off I went to the backyard to do it yet again, while Donna stayed in front, scooping the bountiful snow.

All was going according to standard operating procedure. I carefully inched up the cellar door and grabbed the roof with one hand, firmly planting my L.L.Bean winter boots against the small hinges on the cellar door that allowed it to swing open from the basement. But it turns out that slightly frozen winter boots do not provide surefire grip on an incline involving some slippery Maine snow.

I managed to grab my beloved Frodo in one hand, but in the process of reaching a bit to catch the just-out-of-reach kitty, my big foot started slipping over the top of the small hinge. In a flash, I was sailing back down the cellar door into the deep snow of my backyard, with the cat held high, screaming a very loud "Aaahhh!"

Had she fallen, Frodo would no doubt have adeptly landed on all four feet. But with both of my hands instinctively holding my beloved cat, she had no escape and simply rode down with me. We toppled into the deep Maine snow that had accumulated over the course of the winter.

Donna heard my cry and came racing around the corner of the house, certain my neck or arm or leg was broken. Instead, I had landed unhurt with my heavy jacket into the deep snow, even imprinting the glorious snow angel that was my body shape. Frodo was set down right over the top of my head, with nary a bump or scratch. When Donna arrived, Frodo was standing in the deep snow, looking down at me lying much deeper in the snow (oafs being heavier than cats). She seemed to be pondering our roof exit strategy.

Donna burst out laughing. No one was hurt, and she quickly grasped that I had taken the brunt of the backward fall, holding the cat high and setting her down gently overhead. A Quaker might say that no truer love doth a man show than that he doth falleth from a cellar door for thee.

A journalism student in my American Government class at the University of Maine documented Frodo's roof exploits. Nicole wrote a very sweet article in the student newspaper about my activities as an assistant professor. Entitled "Moen combines teaching and writing, loves both," it was published in the *Maine Campus* on May 1, 1991. Frodo received a brief mention in paragraph two of the story and again near the end in the context of roof traipsing. Nicole quoted me as saying: "My only other full-time sport is getting my cat Frodo off the roof. She climbs a tree near the house ... [and] gets a good view of the neighborhood. Then she is always delighted to see me."

The *Maine Campus* article also mentioned my desire to someday pursue other forms of writing besides scholarship, but hopefully any readers will skip over that part, because the lag time between that comment and this creative non-fiction book just makes me look lazy.

Frodo had jumped from my classroom lectures to the student newspaper, bringing all manner of inquiries for a long time to come. Affiliated with two different universities in my career at this point, Frodo was a mild celebrity at both of them.

Cesarean sections and roof jumping are roads to fame in cat world.

Our inability to stop Frodo from climbing the tree whenever she darn well pleased meant that we often found ourselves standing beneath it, just a second too late to stop her from going up. Across the street, Bud hooted at the two cat-loving Midwesterners standing under their tall tree, spotting their kitty like gymnastics coaches. No further embellishment is required to flesh out the image those words conjure up.

* * *

We had many good times inside the Pearl Street house. Skylights let sunshine in on cold winter days. A mouse-sized office provided

Frodo and me with a quiet place to hang out when I was at home writing books. Brandy entertained us constantly by running wind sprints through the house, up and down the stairs. I envied that he didn't have to duck.

Christmas was an especially great time, when we brought a fresh Maine pine tree into the house. Brandy absolutely loved drinking the sap-infused tree water. Maybe the pulpy taste reminded him of his happy tissue-shredding night in Oklahoma years before. Frodo dragged her catnip presents out from under the tree and started opening them, a wee bit of a protocol violation. Frodo loved catnip mat presents as much as Ralphie loved his Official Red Ryder Carbine-Action Two-Hundred-Shot Range Model Air Rifle in the movie *A Christmas Story*.

Even the incredibly awkward worked out well on Pearl Street. During our three years in that house, Frodo started having more chronic health problems. Her excessive grooming habits were part of the reason, so we started regularly offering her "kitty lube," as we called the over-the-counter hairball medication.

A serious episode occurred when Donna accompanied me to a professional conference in San Francisco. We knew the medicine hadn't worked its magic for several days before we left town, so we mentioned the kitty lube regimen to the college student doing the cat sitting. We plausibly banked on a good outcome, so to speak, but in talking it over with the cat sitter while we were in California, we began to worry that something was awry.

True to form, I fretted about Frodo's health but handed over total responsibility for fixing it to the nurse in my household. She called fellow nurse Chris at the ob-gyn office. An animal lover beyond belief, Chris took her vet-tech friend Michelle along to pay Frodo a house call. The two of them poked and prodded, coming up with a diagnosis of intestinal obstruction.

They said the cat required an enema. A true-to-life Fleet enema purchased at the local pharmacy.

It seems fashionable in the few cat tales I've skimmed through the years to emphasize that Fluffy or Muffy (pick your name) is not a typical cat. You want to talk atypical? Beyond the C-section, the Tide baths, and the head bobbing? Well, top a house call from two health care professionals to give your cat a Fleet enema.

Chris reported to Donna that the procedure was successful, but said Frodo was pretty displeased. Maybe the white princess thought they weren't seeing her best side.

Broadway Veterinary Clinic, where Michelle worked, became our new veterinary clinic. Dr. Ladd had left Brewer Vet, and Michelle was now more familiar with the little white princess than most of us—and than anyone really should be. Besides, Broadway Vet was closer to our Bangor home. No need to travel over the Penobscot River on one of those old or new (or new, new) bridges, always a potential source of confusion.

Once back in town after the conference, where my political science panel had been written up in the *San Francisco Examiner*, Donna and I took Frodo over to Broadway Vet for a full-fledged colon consultation. Talk about hitting some highs and lows.

Dr. Hanks diagnosed Frodo with a mega-colon. Nurse Donna might be able to explain this in far greater detail, but I understood it to be a very large colon that predisposes sufferers to bowel obstructions. Luckily, the condition was manageable.

Donna and I immediately warmed up to Dr. Hanks. He seemed to like Frodo, and he was more than a little amused at the enormously fat medical file we brought with us from Brewer Vet. He somehow knew how to speak Frodo's language, just as Dr. Biles and Dr. Ladd had before him. Best of all, he truly grasped how much she meant to me.

Dr. Hanks did everything he could to treat her maladies, which started mounting as she began her own ascent up the ladder of life.

11

Glencove Castle

I WOKE UP WITH the little white princess staring down at me, inches from my nose. It was a little spooky to wake up and have two fully dilated and round golden eyes staring right at me in the morning. Happened every day, though.

"Hey, wake up, wake up," her body language said. "We're missing the best part of the day. It's almost 5:30 a.m., sleepyhead! Wake up, wake up!"

"Dammit, Frodo," I would mutter while rolling over. "Just give it a rest, would you?"

As I flipped back over on the water bed to get some more shut-eye, Brandy would open one eye or pretend to be fast asleep. He didn't rise as early as Frodo; he liked to stay snuggled with Donna and ride out the water-bed waves until breakfast ended and outdoors time began.

The water bed immobilized Donna like a turtle on its back. She was unable to control her own destiny because every time the heavier person on a water bed shifts, the lightweights involuntarily ride the wave up, then backslide in the direction of the heavier person. Men may have invented the water bed as a subtle mechanism for morning *amore*, as a complementary tactic to telling susceptible cat-loving women hard-luck cat stories. To hold her own, Donna just needed a bigger backside, like Frodo wished.

* * *

There was reason for us to move again. Real estate was slumping badly, so it was the perfect time for the childless, professional couple with steady jobs to move up in the housing market. Our entry-level home was holding its value, especially since we had handsomely paid the contractors to keep the bathroom attached to the rest of the house. We were also weary of enduring Maine's winter snows and summer rains without a garage, and frankly, I was getting damn tired of climbing the cellar door to fetch the white cat off the roof. I'd had no real problems since the one backslide that landed the two of us in the deep snow, but there was always the worry that she would goof up in her leap from the tree to the roof. Cats are supremely self-confident, so foul-ups never cross their minds, but they do happen. I didn't want to witness a rapid descent.

On top of that, we had been having a skunk problem. Not a rabid one, but one Donna mistakenly tried to coax into the house on a dark night when she mistook it for a cat. Through the vet's office, we located the name of a local person who trapped and relocated skunks with his Havahart (have a heart) traps. Out he came in his old pickup with a skunk trap, a blue tarp to put over it to trick the critters, and some peanut-butter crackers to put inside the cage.

We sized one another up.

"I'll charge you after I catch the skunk and relocate it," he said. "I can't really tell you what it costs until then because I don't know how long it will take to catch him. Usually, it isn't too long, especially with peanut butter. They love that stuff."

Payment contingent upon results was enticing, but this also sounded a bit like a former apartment house arrangement. I pressed skunk man a little more for a price, but I still didn't get much of an answer. I rolled over at that point, figuring that almost any price was worth getting rid of the stench. Donna insisted on the Havahart trap approach even for an offending skunk, so this was likely to be expensive.

Problems ensued. Our fearless trapper caught two raccoons, both of which pulled the shiny blue tarp into the cage to shred it. He said that often happened—not really with skunks, but the raccoons were forever pulling the tarps through the wire caging to slice them up.

After some days, our guy caught the offending skunk, drove it five miles into the Maine woods, and set it free. He came back to Pearl Street to settle up. I dreaded the unknown bill.

Before I had a chance to begin what I figured would be an intense negotiation, he piped up, "That will be ten bucks."

Ten bucks. By then, he had stopped by our house the first thing in the morning on any number of days, checking on the traps. He had captured two raccoons and released them into the wild. He had bought replacement tarps. By my count, he was now out considerable time, tarps, crackers, and gas money for his truck to do all this. And yet he proposed charging me only $10.

"Ten bucks?" I said. "You have to be kidding. You're out a lot more than that amount already, and I'm very happy to be rid of the skunk, before something nasty happened."

"Oh, I guess you could give me fifteen then," he replied. "But it doesn't really matter."

"It doesn't really matter?" I repeated.

"No," he said. "It doesn't. I'm not in this for the money. It's just a personal hobby."

It's just a personal hobby.

I thought I had encountered quite a few characters in my time, including the landlady at the Oklahoma apartment complex and the racially motivated furniture salesman by the new bridge. But never before had I run into a guy who relocated skunks as a personal hobby. Talk about an animal lover. He put me to shame; I was just taking care of a single white house cat and her son.

* * *

Exhausting is a good descriptor of our move. The distance from the Pearl Street house to our new house on Glencove Avenue in Bangor was only about a mile, but moving all of our stuff after three years was more arduous because we actually had some worldly possessions this time. Friends helped us, but we mostly made what seemed like a couple thousand trips down Pearl Street, left on Mt. Hope Avenue, and left on Hempstead Avenue onto Glencove. I rather liked living on a street in Maine with "cove" in its name, even if we were forty-five miles from the Atlantic Ocean. It sounded pretty snazzy to a couple of landlubbers from the Great Plains.

Frodo was ready to rock-and-roll every summer day at Glencove Avenue. One of the little-noticed attributes of Maine is that it hangs out there in the North Atlantic on the far edge of the eastern time zone. That's so the state has the same rhythm as the rest of the eastern seaboard. But Maine really should be on Atlantic time, like eastern Canada, because the day grinds to a halt at about 4:00 p.m. during winter. Then, at summer solstice, the sun rises high by 5:00 a.m., which is why Frodo was certain I was already squandering the entire day by still sleeping at 5:30 a.m.

Her other motivation for an early start was moist cat food for breakfast. By now, she had become an almost exclusively moist cat food kitty. For cat owners to have started a feeding routine that involved opening and dishing out a can of moist cat food each new day was right up there in the history of good ideas with Coca-Cola launching "new Coke."

An addict now lived in our house.

"How mannnyyy kitties want some moist food this morning?" is the question I posed each morning. Frodo would be circling my feet, as if to say, "Me, me. I'm one of those kitties who want moist food today." Must be desperate, circling around the large feet of a sleepy oaf.

Brandy was utterly indifferent to food. He only ate when he was walking past the hard cat food en route to someplace else. Born a lone cat into a cornucopia of eight nipples, he never experienced hunger. He nursed until he was almost his mom's size, for goodness' sake. He had never missed a meal, like his mother had, and he never went out of his way to eat. Only a slowly roasting turkey at Thanksgiving truly ignited his passion for food, which we found funny because Frodo on Thanksgiving was typically more interested in the canned turkey giblets than the real thing.

Eventually, I shortened my morning rhetorical question to "How many kitties?" Then it became the even terser "How many?" Frodo always answered enthusiastically to count her in. She possessed a tiny meow but shared it repeatedly on this occasion each day. As time passed, I learned to use this special voice inflection and phrase to bring her running out of hiding. It was a handy tool in a cat lover's arsenal, this ability to summon a furtive feline.

* * *

We moved into a standard raised-ranch house in a lovely Bangor neighborhood—the new kids on the much fancier block. Downstairs, the house on Glencove had a double-car garage, bedroom, family room, and half bath. Upstairs was a combined living room and dining room, a kitchen, two full baths, and three nice bedrooms, including a master bedroom that comfortably held a king water bed, without the fear that it would crash to the floor below. A long hallway from the three bedrooms to the living room gave the kitties a good alley for wind sprinting, and they ran down it all the time. The classic split-level design allowed a cat to sit at the top of the steps and monitor activities ranging from downstairs noise to people walking on the steps, sitting in the living room, or moving down the hallway. Sitting there provided a cat with the same vantage point as the ringmaster enjoyed with Barnum & Bailey.

Frodo warmed up to the place immediately. We had necessarily locked the cats upstairs while finishing up the final trips from Pearl Street to Glencove. The water bed was the last thing to go, but all the while Frodo and Brandy lay on it contently despite the hubbub, awaiting their transfer. They knew they were coming with us. They'd been through this before, and it usually meant an upgrade. Water beds are completely obsolete now. But just as Oldsmobiles might have been repurposed to serve as outdoor cat perches, our cats thought water beds were products that should have been kept. Gently warmed in winter and nicely cooled in summer, a giant water bed was the ultimate cat bedding, so long as a kitty could ride out a few waves with a big guy.

The way Frodo dashed about the new house right from the start made me realize how happy she was to move there. The sellers were incredibly gracious people who left the place spotless when they moved out. Frodo seemed to appreciate the fresh start. Perhaps she held vague recollections of the other places she had lived, where people had brought in fleas.

Her glee was evident as she raced up and down the hall. Her body language said it all: "A castle! A castle! I'm a precious little princess, and now I live in a castle!"

* * *

Frodo's routine varied seasonally. Since only two seasons exist in Maine—winter and non-winter—and winter runs much longer, it deserves treatment first.

Winter mornings were routine par excellence. I hopped out of the heated water bed each morning, usually leaving the sleepier Donna and Brandy to ride out the waves and awake later. After shuffling to fetch my bathrobe in the second bedroom (the wife stole the whole closet of the master bedroom), I bent down to receive the first Frodo rubby of the day. She always trotted ahead of me down the hall, turning her ears (but not her head) to confirm I was following.

Up next was the "how many kitties?" food routine. In response to this daily question, my little princess let out an oh-so-delicate meow. But once the plate hit the floor, the princess acted much more like a cowboy at a chuck wagon. For houseguests who were up early in the morning and took in this sorry spectacle, I typically covered for Frodo by exclaiming, "Wow, she was hungry today!" I was an enabler, a facilitator, or maybe a bit of a liar on this point. But I like to think of my words as simply the gallantry of a man covering for his lady when circumstances warrant.

Next was the dash outdoors. This all started with a Patrick Henry look shot my way—"Give me liberty or give me death." As I started down the steps in the split-level house, Frodo quickly descended right past or between my legs, causing a constant tangle but nary a tumble. She paused at the bottom to monitor my oh-so-painstakingly-slow progress. Perhaps she worried that I was going to forget to open the door and fetch the newspaper for the first time in the zillions of mornings we followed this routine.

Cats are much wiser than dogs when it comes to doors. The average dog sticks its nose behind the door, requiring the human to smack its nose with the door in order to light the dim bulb in the drooling dog's head. Cats simply await the door opening, conserving their drool for personal grooming purposes. Brandy also showed up about then for outside time. On Noah's ark, the animals reportedly loaded up two by two. At Glencove Castle, the cats dashed out in single file, adhering strictly to the seniority principle; Frodo always went first as the dominant cat for this purpose. I'm not sure how the two of them decided which one was dominant when.

Once they were outside, fluffing fresh snow was agenda item number one. Using the snow as a litter box was (pardon the pun) a good number two. While Frodo and Brandy did their thing, I plodded down the driveway for the newspaper. Donna had been drawn to an entirely different house in the area, and I had promised her that if we bought this one, I would be the one to traipse down the driveway each morning to retrieve the local newspaper. Unfortunately for me, women remember this sort of idle pledge.

I dug the newspaper out of our newspaper holder at the end of the driveway and then, as a matter of protocol, always bent down to Frodo's height so she could give it a rubby. Marking the *Bangor Daily News* as a Moen household possession was a major sacrifice; black newsprint doesn't flatter white kitties. Frodo usually scurried behind me as I went back inside, then dashed past me up the stairs for what J. R. R. Tolkien's hobbits would call "second breakfast."

First breakfast was licking up mostly the gravy to gird herself for the plunge into the Maine winter; second breakfast was actually eating some of the giblets. Plates bought on the cheap in San Francisco's Chinatown and shipped back to Maine facilitated second breakfast. We had purchased the set with the idea of using them ourselves, but they hopelessly warped during their first time in a hot dishwasher. Under cat tongue power, the plates facilitated second breakfast by spinning endlessly in circles on the linoleum floor, allowing Frodo to pick off the individual giblets. I came to think of the plates as a lazy Susan for felines.

Frodo kept up the exact same eating routine year-round. She systematically lapped up the juices at first breakfast and ate most of the giblets at second breakfast. She was careful to check for missed morsels.

What followed was a famous Frodo fastidious grooming session in the living room, where a directionally perfect house encouraged the morning sun to stream in the big picture window in the winter. White fur burdens the diligent groomer, much like white gloves owned by the mother-in-law haunted young wives in the sitcoms of old. Stomach, legs, head, tail—every movable body part was involved in the cleaning frenzy. Maybe the spinning lazy Susan had the effect of flinging giblets into her fur.

Once sufficiently clean, Frodo returned for an installment of light cream, which helped with that mega-colon. Milk didn't do the trick, not anymore. Half-and-half? Depended on the day. Light cream was the beverage du jour.

On rare occasions, we would fail to have enough canned gourmet food or light cream in the house. The look of utter disbelief! Frodo had no inclination to accept an explanation. She stood there, stunned, turning up her nose at the Little Friskies with a "what in the hell?" look, and waited until we returned from the convenience store with her goods.

Once she was satiated and clean, it was time to go out the deck door to make sure the backyard looked exactly the same as the last time she saw it. She waltzed over to the door, arched her back, and looked up at the handle. Subtle hint.

A humorous wood sign hung from our deck that read "Beware: Attack Cats." The more appropriate sign probably would have read something like "Happy Cat Lives Here." After all, decks on split-level houses have special appeal to cats because the neighborhood comes into full view. It seems to make absolutely no difference that nothing much happens in a backyard during a Maine winter. Territorial cats simply credit themselves for having everything under control. Among the many species on the earth, only cats congratulate themselves for order in the world when they are seeing, hearing, and doing nothing.

Of course, some Maine winter days were brisk. Frodo's plush coat provided lifesaving protection from the elements, but a cat's comfort calculations are more precisely calibrated than that. Whenever excessive cold or wind hit her face at the deck door, Frodo stopped dead in her tracks. As the freezing air flew up my bathrobe and the electric heat drifted out of the house, she carefully weighed the situation. "Go ahead, honey," I would say, as if my steady encouragement had any relevance to her decision making.

She worked through a complex set of mental calculations, a one-cat Socratic dialogue:

"My face is cold, I'll stay in today."

"No, wait, my butt is warm. I'll go out."

"No, wait, *hate* cold, *love* warm. I'll stay in."

"No, wait, haven't been in the backyard today. Must check it out."

"No, wait, I was already in the front yard today. Close enough. I'll stay in."

"No, wait, was that today?"

As my genitals starting forming icicles and as Central Maine Power eyed a lien on my property for the cost of the electric heat, Frodo leapt out on the deck with reckless abandon, akin to a kamikaze pilot.

She took pretty much one full step into the cold with nose lifted to inhale and verify the cold temperature. Then came a swift pirouette back into the house. Then a testy look shot my way that said, "Dumb bunny. You could have warned me."

I learned to shrug it off and just hold the door handle while she ran through her mental gymnastics. The real winner on those cold days was L.L.Bean, as I bought their flannel nightshirts and boxers to cut down on the chill. I should have bought stock in the local utility company too.

One winter day, all of the backyard ritual was turned upside down. The day started out normally, with the roll out of bed, first breakfast, retrieving the newspaper, second breakfast, and cat bath. Then came Frodo's time to hit the backyard. The snow was deep and glazed with a very thin layer of ice from the night before, but the emerging day was sunny and pleasant.

I let Frodo onto the deck after her usual hemming and hawing. Sensing the gradually warming temperature, she walked down the snowy deck steps and into the backyard. Surveying the landscape and seeing nothing out of the ordinary, I closed the deck door and started making a cup of freshly brewed coffee. New England was not Seattle, but I had become an aficionado of grinding my own coffee beans. Frodo would likely retreat to underneath the deck, where the snow was less deep. Then she would no doubt come back up the steps to be let in. I figured I had a few minutes to brew and sip my coffee.

I was holding a cup of steaming coffee, standing in my red L.L.Bean flannel pajamas, with my back toward the deck, when arose the loud shrieking of two cats about to rumble. I knew this pattern, one of increasingly strident yowls and much head tilting. The scenario where cat number one conveys to cat number two, "You suck." Cat number two replies with "You suck more." Cat number one shoots back, "No, you really, really suck the most of all." Finally, cat number two reiterates the same phrase, but with even more embellishment.

Hearing the yowling, I stepped quickly toward the deck door with my sipped-upon cup of coffee still in my hands and my sleepy eyes still struggling to focus. Seconds mattered in averting these fights. Cats often hemmed and hawed about fighting, preferring rhetorical insults to actual combat. If one could interrupt the intense stares and the unfriendly arguing between the enemy cats, usually they would break off before any real damage occurred.

Saving Frodo before she did her "hiss, run, and get slashed" routine was my objective.

Rushing out the door to yell or to pound the deck to head off the fight, I spied the two enemy cat combatants just a short distance from the bottom of the deck stairs. Instinctively, I dashed down the steps, figuring that in case the yelling didn't work, the thundering noise of a gigantic Viking descendent would cause the cats to break the standoff. About halfway down the steps, with my coffee still in hand but now spilling over the sides of the cup, my feet started sliding. Facing a split-second decision, I chose to dive forward into the snow ahead of me, rather than risk falling backward onto the hard steps behind me.

What both cats witnessed was quite different. They saw a big clod running down the steps, voluntarily diving forward into the snow, tossing his coffee cup high in the air with brown liquid flying everywhere, and instinctively screaming "Whoaaa!" as he took flight. On the still winter day, my voice probably carried beyond the neighborhood and into the greater Bangor/Brewer region.

As I struggled to first right and then reorient myself, I glimpsed two cats staring at me in utter disbelief. Enemy cat was thinking of only one word—*dipshit*. Even my beloved Frodo had to be thinking, *Love you, big guy, but that was way beyond humiliating.*

Frodo probably experienced flashbacks of the cellar door on Pearl Street. She realized that these oafs populating the world were prone to fall either backward or forward, with or without kitties. These oafs were airborne more often than one would think.

Donna heard me scream as I went down, and she came flying out the deck door, again thinking my arms, legs, or neck were shattered. Instead, there I stood with snow smashed into my ears and covering my glasses, wedged solidly between the lenses and my eyes. Knee-deep in snow, I stood surrounded by brown coffee stains on the beautiful white flakes, with a wide pattern of dispersal and just a hint of running liquid melting into the snow where the steaming coffee met up with the icy glaze.

The two kitties declared a truce so they could fully assimilate in their little cat brains the spectacle caused by the fierce Viking descendent. One could almost hear them ask, "Really, these are the guys who struck terror into the hearts of European villagers for two centuries?"

Catfight? Averted. Human dignity? Lost.

12

Pouncing Pigeons, Maddening Mouse

WORK OFTEN TOOK CENTER stage as I steadily rose through the ranks of the professoriate at the University of Maine. Teaching classes and writing books constituted my favorite activities, but a couple of members of the Department of Political Science pushed me toward academic administration a bit earlier than usual. Serving as chairperson was time consuming and much more of a headache than being a professor, but it was rewarding working on behalf of others, mostly a great bunch of dedicated teachers and scholars.

A few years as chairperson, and I suddenly held a second position as special assistant to the president at the University of Maine. A different career started to take shape, one separate from the stereotype of the pipe-smoking, plaid-wearing professor.

What happened on the home front on a typical day with the kitty cats while I was up the road at UM was a mystery. A good guess would be that an exhausting morning ritual was followed by long hours of sleep. Cat books report that felines sleep 80 percent of the day. Cat owners know that reported percentage is absurd. No cat can possibly stay awake the other 20 percent of the day, unless it is young.

Regrettably, Frodo was no longer young. She was probably a year old when she walked into my life, and she had now lived more than a decade. Advancing age showed in subtle ways. More kitty lube and light cream were needed to attain the same intestinal results. A fluid-filled cyst on her head required Dr. Hanks to perform minor surgery. (Donna couldn't resist the jokes about the lobotomy for my blonde kitty.) A mild thyroid deficiency required some monitoring, but nothing else. Allergies and sneezing occurred in late spring and early summer. Life's cruel irony, recognized by all, is that as we increase our ability to enjoy life, through greater material wealth and broader perspective, we face a shorter distance to the end.

I have spoken little of my feelings in recent pages, preferring to describe Frodo's goofy exploits. A Scandinavian predisposition to be tight-lipped is part of the reason, but it is more the pain of describing the slow decline of a beloved companion. Pets occupy a special place in our hearts because they offer love without reservation. And cats especially, because they live life to its fullest without complaint. They provide laughs, bring people closer together, warm up the household, and on a good day, eradicate a few mice. Cats can't rise to the level of humans, but they don't descend into pettiness or ill will. They never lose their heart or spirit, even as their strength and agility fade. Always for me Frodo had that spark and love in her eyes.

In turn, I am convinced that we endear ourselves to them. As Frodo gradually aged, I traded in my initial role as nurturing mother for that of protective father. Whenever Frodo went outside for any length of time, I tried to head out too. The neighbors laughed. So did the vet when he heard about it. I patrolled the property while Frodo was outside, toying with things in the yard or driveway while keeping a watchful eye on her. Initially disdainful, she later seemed to appreciate the security blanket, especially when Brandy wasn't out. She paraded around the neighborhood with complete confidence, even losing her lifetime fear of dogs.

Evening rituals reinforced our changed relationship. Frodo always met me at the door of the garage, bounding down the stairs of the split-level house when she heard the familiar electric garage door. I extended my fingers for the "my, I haven't seen you for a long time" double (or sometimes even triple) rubby.

After that, Frodo shot upstairs, showing me the way to the kitchen. "Yoo-hoo, come this way," she silently implored, as if I would forget to head up the stairs myself. We finished off the "how many kitties?" routine, then often plunked down on the sofa together on the dark winter nights. Frodo s-t-r-e-t-c-h-e-d to her maximum length to promote the best possible tummy rub, often looking over her shoulder to gaze back at me and purr.

* * *

Frodo's summer routine was different from her winter routine. With the University of Maine out for the summer, my daily schedule became more flexible. Frodo consumed much of my time outdoors, in part because I sadly sensed the situation between us was now changing more rapidly, the gap between life cycles showing. I wanted to hang around her more. For her part, perhaps she figured she was helping keep me occupied for the summer. *Oh, he seems to be doing just fine on his own in the winter,* she may have thought, *but he still seems to be unemployed in the summer.*

She nearly gave my dear father a fatal heart attack well before his time. Mom and Dad were visiting us in Maine, as they often did in the summers before heading down to Boston to see my brother, Mike, then to New Jersey to see my sister Mary. We were sharing one of those lovely Maine summer mornings on the deck over coffee.

We had already completed the first breakfast/outdoors/second breakfast/bathing ritual, so the two kitties were sitting on the back deck with us, bird-watching. Brandy totally sat this one out, but not Frodo. She knew if she scored one of those pigeons for the family freezer, she would be a hero for the rest of the summer, especially given the apparently unemployed goober.

Aahhh, pigeons. Big, fat, juicy pigeons. Cooing, clucking, warbling pigeons. Heads that steadily bobbed, much like a cat overdosed on over-the-counter worm medicine. And so many pigeons too, right in the neighbor's yard behind us.

Succulent birdies, thought Frodo.

The hunt was on. First, the all-knowing hunting look appeared on her face, followed by a rapid descent down the deck steps. Not as rapidly as I went down the steps that one winter day, mind you, but much sleeker and more stylish. No pitiful screaming. No coffee splashing.

Once on the grass, Frodo dropped down into the kitty slink, that low-to-the-ground, tail-down, tummy-dragging crawl across an open area. Honed over the course of centuries by lions on the African plains in search of unsuspecting zebra, the slink seems a little over the top for fat suburban kitties, but perhaps not to the individual slinker.

A row of bushes marked the property line. Frodo managed to duck behind one of those bushes. She needed to move two bushes over to have a realistic chance at a succulent pigeon.

As we witnessed this hunt unfold from our perch on the deck, we were pretty sure that every single pigeon in the flock watched the kitty slink to the next bush. The entire flock of warbling pigeons lit out as she moved to that next bush.

Frodo obviously heard and saw the pigeons filling the skies, but even a single straggler meant that pigeon breast was still on the menu. We watched her gather all of her strength and lay back her ears. She went into the famous kitty rump wiggle, the time when the cat alerts all of his or her fast-twitch muscles to kick in simultaneously, accompanied by an adrenaline surge.

Perhaps she was too enveloped in the heat of the moment, or maybe the picture wasn't clear until she was out and around the bush she was hiding behind. With a mental rallying cry of "Death to the pigeons!" the white kitty hurled herself toward the one laggard green pigeon.

Yes, a green pigeon.

Frodo pounced on the neighbor's plastic lawn sprinkler. Unfortunately, sprinklers do more to keep grass green than cats fat. And Frodo had thought it embarrassing when I crashed down the deck steps. Good grief—this was even more humiliating.

My father with the heart condition laughed so hard that the rest of us split our time between laughing uncontrollably and monitoring his breathing. Jokes followed. The wife reprised her dumb-blonde jokes, followed by dumb-cat jokes, exchanged so many times over by witnesses to the incident. What could I say? My only play was to be like the mysterious voice at the start of *Mission: Impossible* episodes and disavow any knowledge of the actions.

On your own, babycakes, I thought, turning my back on Frodo for the first time since the cooking aunts had booted her out of the kitchen for misconduct so long ago.

* * *

But nothing was weirder than Mighty Mouse. Each summer, I stacked small amounts of split wood in the garage to dry so the pieces would be ready for the fireplace in winter. While standing in the garage one summer day, taking stock of our inventory, Donna and I watched a mouse pop right out of the woodpile. Not just any mouse, but one with chutzpah.

The cats saw it too.

Stunned by their good fortune, Frodo and Brandy dashed to the spot where the mouse ducked in after his little loop-the-loop. Seconds later, he reappeared a little farther down, but only for a brief instant before vanishing back into the woodpile.

Donna and I figured this mouse was inadvertently trapped in the garage, so we each picked up a kitty, with the idea of herding the mouse out the open garage doors. The cats were wiggly and pissed, especially because the mouse showed no desire to leave. It kept popping out of the woodpile to run in quick circles, with no regard for anything. We set the cats back down, thinking some Darwinian natural selection was probably in order. Donna dashed for the camera to get a picture of the cats watching Mighty Mouse; they seemed to be more mesmerized by the rodent than interested in dusting him.

Again and again, the mouse reemerged, running so close to Brandy on one pass that the cat picked up his foot to let the mouse by. Brandy sniffed the rodent and retched. Something was seriously wrong with this mouse, and the cats knew it. Mighty Mouse was deranged.

When that fact sunk in, we swiftly picked up the cats and put them in the house. They vigorously protested this too—a mouse, even a kooky mouse, is worth monitoring, and possibly eating. But their protests were lame. They had already passed on ample opportunities to munch that mouse, reminding me of the big-talking Cowardly Lion in *The Wizard of Oz*.

This episode ended badly and ironically. Passionate animal lover Donna inadvertently quashed the life of the roundabout rodent. We had herded Mighty Mouse into the driveway with considerable effort after he ran out of the woodpile, but as he circled back toward the garage, he made a beeline for Donna's feet. She had an empty cardboard box in hand to trap him in, but in the panic of having a mouse run straight at her, she missed ever so slightly, accidentally breaking a little leg. Tears welling in her eyes, she begged me to finish off the crippled fellow while she looked away.

This should be the only instance in my life where I have to murder an insane rodent.

Wayward cat pounces and funny mice were part of the charm of life at the Glencove Castle. Many times I sat outside on the deck with Frodo, doing nothing but sitting with her. I did this more and more as I noticed her minor health problems mounting and accelerating. We watched and listened to the world around us, spending many unhurried minutes together. She had life's necessities and major pleasures—comfort, security, and love. I kept her safe outdoors, and Donna stumbled across grilled teriyaki beef (supposedly for us) to please her palate. She enjoyed long tummy rubs while she stretched out on my legs in an L.L.Bean deck chair. She was no damsel in distress, held against her will; she was the reigning queen of the Glencove Castle.

13

The Kingsville Motel

THE SWEEPING TURN AT Omaha, Nebraska, transferred me from I-29 south to I-80 east toward Chicago. The good news—Sioux Falls was now 140 miles behind me. But still ahead of me were 1,600 miles to Bangor. The accelerator was pushed as hard as I dared.

I wasn't stopping for meals because Mom had sent along sandwiches and fruit. In fact, for this trip Mom had outfitted me with more provisions than I'd need to climb Mount Everest.

I was driving my used Chrysler New Yorker, purchased from Mom and Dad. It was a richly appointed vehicle, loaded with every electronic gizmo imaginable. Its prize feature for a man in a hurry was an overhead digital console that reliably reported the exact number of miles to empty. I could run the car down to almost nothing before stopping to pump gas.

Dad bought a new car, and we had concluded a deal for this one. Had he thought of it, he might have charged me more than the car's book value and put the excessive profit toward new screens for his house windows. Many second thoughts raced through my head as I sped down the highway, but none of them about the car. Instead, I kept questioning my decision to drive back to Bangor, replaying the precise sequence of events over and over in my mind.

* * *

I had been back in South Dakota for three fun-filled weeks, my longest time there since moving to Maine. I had purchased a surprisingly cheap one-way plane ticket so I could drive the used Chrysler New Yorker back to Maine. What a change from the bleak days of purple Gremlins with blue-jean seats.

The signature event of this trip was my twentieth high-school reunion. I planned to stay in South Dakota through Father's Day, coming as it did right on the heels of the class reunion. Sons who love their dads don't miss opportunities to be with them on their special day.

Friday evening was great fun. Washington High was the oldest and largest of the Sioux Falls high schools, the academic home of many of the state's future leaders. As part of the baby boom generation, I had graduated in a class of almost 600 students. We spent the night before the reunion dinner getting together at an informal party thrown by some of our classmates. We renewed old friendships and had those awkward conversations with spouses we were meeting for the first time—the ones where as a reunion participant, you are trying to be nice while not really wanting to waste your limited time on new faces. In turn, the new faces are standing bravely and loyally alongside a classmate all night, wishing they were instead swinging from a noose.

Back in Maine, nearly three weeks after I flew to South Dakota, the little white princess wandered into the family room in the basement late in the evening. According to Donna, who is necessarily the storyteller, Frodo jumped onto the couch, trembled slightly, and then plopped down next to her to rest, breathing heavily. This was definitely uncharacteristic behavior. The nurse quickly sensed a serious health issue. Her worst fear was something happening to Frodo while I was away, and this seemed to be it.

Donna called Broadway Vet at about 10:00 p.m., begging yet again to have Frodo seen after normal business hours. Dr. Benson—the major partner in the practice—graciously agreed because of the labored breathing described by the nurse. Veterinarians took Donna seriously because she combined a love of animals with medical knowledge. And they knew she didn't panic. Nurses in charge of labor and delivery floors cannot afford to panic.

Donna rushed Frodo to the vet. His initial diagnosis was a severe asthmatic attack. This was consistent with Frodo's symptoms and her increased allergies as she aged. Specific triggers remained elusive, which was troublesome. Just as a precaution, Dr. Benson insisted on keeping Frodo overnight for observation and oxygen.

Donna called Dr. Benson first thing the next morning, expecting to hear about Frodo's recovery. Instead, she received unwelcome, almost grim, news. Frodo's breathing had become even more labored during the night. Her pulse weakened. Her eyes lost some of their shine. Worried about her swift decline, Dr. Benson conducted middle-of-the-night tests. This all resulted in a new and potentially serious diagnosis—hypertrophic cardiomyopathy. In layman's terms, a critically enlarged heart with a potentially lethal outcome.

And there I sat, more than 1,700 miles away, with a breaking heart and a newly purchased Chrysler New Yorker rather than an airplane ticket to take me home.

* * *

As Donna agonized over Frodo's deteriorating condition, I was oblivious. My lifelong friend Steve and I went to the graduation party early and stayed late, munching on snacks, drinking beer, and engaging others in conversation.

Donna had called Mom earlier in the day, right after learning of Frodo's critical heart problems. But after much discussion, they decided to withhold the information from me because it was the day of the actual reunion and there wasn't much I could do from halfway across the continent. Yes, Frodo had suffered a serious health setback, but she was likely to improve now that she was receiving care for a diagnosed problem. What difference did one day make?

They made the wrong decision, of course. At least, it has always seemed wrong to me. Regardless, they made a tough decision designed to protect me, as those who love others often do. Their subsequent anguish was palpable.

I arrived back at my folks' house in the wee hours. Mom greeted me at the door, which caught me a little off-guard. I was almost forty years old, so I was more than a little humored by the thought of my mom staying up to meet me after a night on the town. Who even knew motherhood was so tiring?

Once a mom, always a mom, I thought to myself.

She managed a weak smile when she met me at the back door, but then cut right to the chase. "Call home right away," she said. "Donna is expecting it."

Even funnier—having to check in with the wife after a reunion event attended by a few old high-school sweethearts. This was quaint, even cute.

"But it is very late, Mom," I protested. "I'll just call her in the morning. You can verify that I came home in good shape." I grinned at my own late-night wit.

Mom brushed aside my words. "I *know* the time," she said, "but Donna is expecting a call from you, so just do it." With that, she turned and walked out of the room.

This was weird. My mother isn't a leave-the-room sort of person, especially after going to the trouble of staying up until the wee hours of the night to tell me to call home. As I started dialing my home number, my stomach started churning. Not a good combination, this light alcohol and nervousness. The old "no matter what time it is" telephone call almost always connotes sickness—in this case, probably not involving Donna, since she was the one awaiting the call.

I have no clear recollection of my conversation with her. Perhaps the hour was too late, the alcohol was heavier than I thought, or the news of Frodo's condition was too much to absorb. All I can really remember is a tearful wife quietly saying over and over again, "I'm so sorry, honey." She hurt for Frodo, and she hurt for me. And she hurt badly for not telling me sooner.

What an awful feeling on my end to know that Frodo had been whisked to the vet now some twenty-four hours earlier. That was the part they hadn't thought through when they decided not to tell me. While I celebrated, Frodo struggled. While I lived it up, Frodo fought to live. Guilt sank in just thinking about it. Why was I not blessed with the intuition to know something was wrong?

Numbly, I sat in the basement, wanting to stay awake to fully digest the grim news, while fully aware that I sorely needed some sleep. My heart ached knowing that I was giving Frodo my least when she needed me most. But just what could I do at 3:00 a.m. on a Saturday night with my liver metabolizing? No planes were flying. It was no time to be driving. No options existed. Thinking about my beloved cat's health and replaying this nasty sequence of events in my mind, I fell into a fitful sleep.

* * *

Donna called me again the next morning, on Father's Day, not too many hours after our late-night conversation. She had talked Dr. Benson into letting her visit Frodo first thing on Sunday morning, and now she was calling with an update.

She presented distinctly mixed news. Frodo's breathing had improved considerably, due to her sitting in an oxygen tent for this long. On the other hand, a medication administered to ease the cardiomyopathy seemed to be doing little good. And liver function tests suggested the possibility of liver disease in addition to a heart condition. Our long-standing practice—upon the advice of a vet— to give her part of a baby aspirin every other day had greatly eased her arthritis but evidently taken a toll on her liver. The dog that had caused the arthritis by twisting her leg when she was a pregnant stray was coming back to bite her a second time.

Furthermore, her appetite was waning. She had yet to eat during her time at the vet's office in the oxygen tent. It wasn't like my "how many kitties?" cat to pass on food, but I told myself that these were extenuating circumstances. Donna tried a different food each time she visited—favorite cat food, Kentucky Fried Chicken, and even grilled teriyaki beef. No luck.

Despite the negative signs, Dr. Benson thought Frodo could regain her strength. She would just have to live a more sedate life. She would be weaker, and heart medication would have to be administered. She might become more arthritic too, because we would have to dial back on the baby aspirin.

How long would she live? It all depended on the rate of enlargement, the efficiency of the heart pumping. Later that morning, Dr. Benson called a fellow vet with the equipment to perform an echocardiogram. Unfortunately, it being Father's Day, the male vet was unavailable for the day. An appointment was set up through his answering service for the next morning. Donna volunteered to transport Frodo from one office to the other so the test could be done the very first thing the next day.

Donna sobbed when she called me again. Arrangements to evaluate Frodo further were now locked into place, but Dr. Benson had also broached the possibility that she might not make it. Donna implored me to take the first available plane home.

I resisted her advice for both irrational and practical reasons. The irrational reason was anger—kept in the dark about Frodo's situation for more than twenty-four hours, I was now being asked to hop a plane home, leaving behind a car and my father on Father's Day. On the practical side, only Northwest Airlines connected Sioux Falls with Bangor. I telephoned them and found out a one-way, same-day ticket cost hundreds of dollars. Northwest representatives had heard many a sob story and cared little about a passenger hoping to fly home for a sick cat.

While this was not cost prohibitive, the logistics were complex. I would have to buy another ticket back to Sioux Falls to return with the New Yorker to Maine. When I would be able to get back to Sioux Falls was unclear, dependent on Frodo's rate of recovery and my own summer schedule. Meanwhile, we would be down one car at home. Besides, flying from a small airport in Sioux Falls to another small airport in Bangor took about eight hours. It guaranteed nothing. Already, it was into the early afternoon on Father's Day. The very best I could do was fly out in a couple more hours, connecting in Minneapolis and Boston. Frodo might die ten minutes after I bought the expensive plane ticket, or I could end up stuck in either of those two major hubs, since I was catching the last flights out. Even well-intentioned flying could be for naught.

Moreover, Frodo was still in the oxygen tent at Broadway Vet, awaiting transport the next morning to the other vet for the echo-cardiogram. I wouldn't arrive in Bangor until 11:00 p.m. on Sunday night on Father's Day. It was unlikely that the vet's office would open to let me see Frodo after Donna had already bent their rules so many times. What was the point of rushing home if I couldn't even see her when I arrived?

Abruptly leaving my sixty-eight-year-old father on Father's Day wasn't easy either. Four children scattered across the country, and I was the only one anywhere near him on his special day. He said to go ahead, but leaving on his day seemed unfair.

Driving also presented problems. Two consecutive evenings of high-school reunion parties had left me exhausted. And I'd gotten very little sleep the night before, after I learned of Frodo's illness. My nerves would be frazzled while on the road, and in this era before cell phones, I would be incommunicado with everyone. Loved ones admonished me not to drive so far while weary and worried.

Donna and I talked through various scenarios, none of which suggested an immediate departure from South Dakota, even though I longed to arrive at Frodo's side. Logic dictated that we do nothing until Dr. Benson examined her again, which he promised to do later in the afternoon. I tried my best at napping while awaiting the next call from Donna, so that I would be rested for travel of some kind, but of course I couldn't sleep a wink.

Events had conspired: the reunion in South Dakota, the cat's weekend illness, Father's Day, the lack of timely flights, ownership of a Chrysler New Yorker. Then events took still another bad turn. Dr. Benson faced an emergency case of a bleeding animal that af-ternoon. He examined Frodo, but later than expected. By the time Donna had a medical update, my window of opportunity to buy an expensive plane ticket and catch the final flights out on Father's Day had closed. Driving was now the only option, but it seemed pointless since I wouldn't make it much beyond Omaha before darkness started to descend.

Frodo was in an oxygen tent fighting for her life. An entire day had been spent waiting, not knowing, not deciding, second-guessing—and leading absolutely nowhere. I was not one single mile closer to home.

Now it only made sense to await the results of the echocardiogram scheduled for the next morning at the other vet's office. But I also booked a flight to leave the next afternoon on those same flights if the echocardiogram indicated big trouble. I held off on the actual purchase, just guaranteeing the reservation with a credit card for twenty-four hours, as one could do in those days. This strategy left open the next-day possibility of catching a plane or jumping in the New Yorker and driving like hell. I filled the gas tank and packed all my belongings so I could leave in an instant. Having fully prepared for each scenario, I quietly contemplated the likelihood of making it home in time to say good-bye, fought back tears on Father's Day, and waited out another painfully long night.

* * *

Donna called mid-morning on Monday, following the procedure. The echocardiogram showed significant enlargement and irreparable damage to Frodo's heart. The vet gave her little chance for recovery, but he expected her to live for some time on heart medication or for about ten days if she didn't improve.

Donna gently relayed the crushing news.

Absent a miracle, Frodo's life was winding down. I could do nothing about it. After a dozen years together—marked by so much love and hundreds of memories—our time together was ending, our paths diverging. Tears streamed freely down my cheeks at being so far away.

There was nothing left to do but race home to see her. The good news—if it could be called that—was two vets agreeing that she would stay alive for a time. I would be able to hold her in my arms yet again. She might be able to leave this earth in my loving embrace, my only consolation.

Donna and I discussed flying and driving all over again. She pushed hard for flying, just in case. But this was my call, and I chose to drive, for all the same reasons as before. Although Frodo might not recover, she was likely to hang on for a while longer, under vet care.

Strong was the sense that I would make it back in time.

My secret weapon was adrenaline. Once on the road, nothing would stop me. Packed with provisions, I backed out of the driveway late on Monday morning within a few minutes of hanging up the phone. I sped down I-29.

* * *

My own Indy 500 is how I thought about this trip. This wouldn't be the scenic saunter over the Trans-Canada Highway that had brought all of us to Maine, but the straightest shot and quickest route on the fastest American highways. Total driving time ranged from twenty-four to thirty hours. I banked on something less than the low estimate.

At least I was getting a late-morning start, which meant many hours of daylight ahead because it was almost the summer solstice. It was so hard to think of death in such a season of bountiful sunshine and life.

My original plan was thirteen hours of driving, then pulling off the road about midnight. I'd sleep a few hours at some roadside hotel, I figured, and then drive the rest of the way. If all went according to plan, I would be home by Tuesday evening, about a day and a half after the echocardiogram showing heart damage. The vet who had performed the heart tests had guessed Frodo would last at least ten days, I reminded myself, so this should work.

Making it a race helped considerably. I moved at a brisk clip, just as fast as common sense allowed. Speeding pumped adrenaline through my body, and that helped with the sheer exhaustion of re-union parties and heartbreaking news. More than anything, racing provided a comforting distraction. At last, at long last—after so much waiting and wondering what to do—I was driving as fast as I dared in order to get back for a heartbreaking good-bye to the cat of my life.

Over and over in my head, the same refrain: *Hold on, Frodo. I'm coming.* And all along, I sensed that I would make it, that this crazy sequence of events ultimately would be overcome. Deep down, I even hoped that Frodo might rally once we reunited. She could draw strength from my love. A miracle might happen.

I ran the digital indicator to as low as eight miles before stopping to fill the car up with gas. Each time was like a pit stop at a raceway. I jumped out of the car to fill it, partly to recharge myself, then grabbed a thinly brewed Midwestern coffee and quickly accelerated back into traffic to resume the adrenaline rush. These intermittent stops broke the monotony. I also scanned radio stations, listened to recorded music, pushed electronic gizmo buttons, and sang along to stay alert. Any trick to keep driving east at full tilt.

The Iowa-Illinois border was eight hours into my journey. Just one brief stop so far, for gas. Dark clouds loomed on the horizon. This seemed like a perfect opportunity to stretch my legs and call Donna to ask how things were going, before I plunged into the bad weather and Chicago traffic. I dialed a whole bunch of calling-card numbers. No small talk this time.

"Hi, sweetie, how is she doing?" I asked.

"Oh, Matt, I don't know," Donna said. "But I think better. She is resting comfortably. I only hope I did the right thing."

"What's that?" I queried.

"I brought her home," Donna replied quietly.

"You did? You brought her home? How come?" I asked. My obvious fear was so that Frodo could die at home.

Donna explained. While Frodo was recuperating back in the vet's oxygen tent from the morning echocardiogram, Donna was assembling all of the necessary gear to bring her home. She thought it best because she could give the cat full attention. Only a cat lover and a nurse could have arranged this. Donna begged, borrowed, pleaded, and rented everything necessary to set up an oxygen tent at home, with help from the kindly Dr. Benson.

She monitored Frodo's respirations and heart rate with her own stethoscope.

Donna worried about whether she had done the right thing while I was on the road and unable to be consulted. Of course she had, I firmly assured her. In fact, this was great because it would probably give Frodo added strength and willpower. One additional move was more than offset by having Frodo in the comfort of her own home, where she could rest peacefully and quietly, with the heart medication working its magic to prolong her life. Donna took a day off from work to make it happen. And now Frodo would be home when I arrived the next day.

The news lifted my heart and buoyed my spirits.

I was so thankful. Donna was doing everything humanly possible, and even things that seemed impossible, like a cat oxygen tent at home. This topped even Tide baths and an enema by two medical professionals in its improbability.

"Why don't you say something to her," Donna suggested, "so she can at least hear your voice. You've been gone so long." She held the phone up in the direction of Frodo's ears, even as the cat rested in the tent.

A strange moment for the social scientist on the other side of the telephone receiver, but I plunged right in. "Hang in there, honey," I cooed to her. "I'm on my way. I'm coming as fast as I can." She knew my voice, and she knew the essence of those words and that inflection. She had heard soft words from me so many times in her life, and I hoped they would give her some more fighting spirit.

I hung up the phone and ran back to the car. Again, I accelerated into the traffic stream, this time relatively joyous. Frodo was home where she belonged. She was resting comfortably, helped by medication and oxygen. A private-duty nurse watched her like a hawk. And now I was almost one-third of the way home. A realistic chance to say good-bye, and a long shot that this might even turn around a bit when I got home, if only for a time. This dark situation was suddenly looking much brighter.

* * *

But Chicago was a complete nightmare. Heavy rain and summer construction brought traffic to a crawl as I tried to skirt the Windy City on I-80. Trucks pounded my windshield with splashed water, straining my tired eyes further. Chicago was ten hours from Sioux Falls, and on a rainy evening, the last of the daylight was quickly dissipating. The slow pace took its toll on my body. I wondered if it was wise to pull off and sleep a little now while it rained, with the thought of going the rest of the way once it let up.

No, I better get at least halfway, I told myself. With that thought, I kept pushing toward Indiana.

Before long, my spirits rose again. As Chicago faded away in my rearview mirror, traffic dropped off and the weather improved. I hung closely behind several trucks that were barreling down the highway, suggesting the coast was clear. I breezed through skinny Indiana and started looking ahead to Cleveland in a couple more hours. Feeling good with the wide-open road laid out in front of me, I began flirting with going all the way to Maine. Unstoppable momentum.

I studied the map under the car light while racing down the highway in the pitch dark. Exactly the type of thing my loved ones on both ends of the trip were so concerned about, but nothing happened. I could see that driving right through Cleveland rather than around it shaved off miles. Doing so would allow me to clear one of the last urban areas on the way to Maine.

Okay, I thought to myself, *at least land someplace east of Cleveland. That's better than halfway. It gets me around tomorrow morning's traffic. If I'm still moving along at a good clip, maybe I'll head for the Pennsylvania border.*

I zipped through an empty downtown Cleveland at about 2:30 a.m., now having driven some 900 miles since leaving Sioux Falls. I had hardly been out of the car; my back and neck ached right along with my heart.

But still I kept going. The middle of night was the best time to pound through the states of the industrial Midwest. Light traffic, no road construction. Trucks on the road for those very reasons, running interference for me. I kept pushing the accelerator.

I was overdue to telephone Donna; our last call had been hours ago, back in Iowa. I needed to tell her my location and let her know that I was making terrific progress en route home. I was also anxious to hear the latest news on Frodo's medical condition, although the last report had immeasurably boosted my spirits. Part of the reason

I hadn't called was the simple calculation that I could stop to call about a situation beyond my control or I could just drive to get there. On this one, I again trusted my instincts. *Just get home,* I thought to myself, *just get home.* Frodo and I would spend our remaining days together in the beautiful Maine summer.

Jeez, would I pamper her! Thinking about just how much brought a smile to my face. Teriyaki beef would be the new "chicken in every pot" of the Great Depression days.

Then the trip took a turn for the worse. I left behind the rain in Illinois, but a new batch of rain found me as I started to traverse Ohio. And what a horrendous rain—an absolute Great Lakes summer deluge. Truckers began pulling off the road in the wee hours before the sunrise to let the storm blow through while they rested. For a time, I slowed down to a paltry forty miles per hour so I could see the road ahead. I kept on pushing, but it became increasingly pointless because progress was so slow. And weariness was overtaking me. I had to be rested enough to finish off the drive the next day. Better to knock off for a few hours and shoot to Maine on dry roads in the full light of day. I pulled off in North Kingsville, Ohio, at the aptly named Kingsville Motel.

* * *

A very crabby elderly lady answered the bell that I pressed at about 4:15 a.m. on that Tuesday morning. She must have been the mom of this mom-and-pop motel. She willingly rented me a room but refused to wake up much to do so. She completed the transaction, tossed a key on the counter, and trudged back to bed. My own reserves exhausted, I also shuffled off to my room.

I collapsed on the bed for a few minutes to clear my head and rest my aching back. But knowing that if I lay down for too long I would be fast asleep, I made myself get back up and walk out into the driving rain to fetch my bag, forgotten because of weariness. I had driven almost 1,000 miles, virtually nonstop, from South Dakota to the Pennsylvania border. Donna would no doubt yell at me for this stunt when I called her.

I peeled off the rain-soaked clothes, went into the bathroom, and drank several glasses of water, figuring it could hit bottom while I was sleeping in a hotel with a bathroom. Such pre-planning might save a stop or two tomorrow, and many hours on the road had left me dehydrated. I quickly ran a toothbrush around my teeth. The Kingsville Motel was just what a weary traveler needed.

I pulled out the calling card again with all of the numbers and started pressing the digits to reach Donna. She answered on the second ring.

"Hi, honey," I started out. "I know it's very late, but I wanted to let you know that I've made great progress and I'm just fine, parked in some hotel at the Ohio-Pennsylvania border. Everything is okay. How is Frodo doing?"

A long pause followed.

A very long pause followed.

Uh-oh, I thought to myself, *I'm going to get yelled at for driving too far in one day. Maybe I shouldn't have told her just how far I raced down the highway.*

"Matt, where have you been?" she asked. Hmm, I sensed more hell than I'd thought for not checking in earlier. But she had to be pleased to know just how far I'd made it. With 1,000 miles now behind me, pulling into Bangor tomorrow evening was entirely realistic. All I needed was a few hours of sleep to pave the way.

Then before I could even reply to her rhetorical question, Donna quietly uttered the crushing words that proved my gut feelings so very wrong.

"I'm so sorry," Donna said as her voice cracked. "Frodo died a few hours ago. I kept hoping all night long that you would call before it happened so you could say good-bye."

In an instant, this great race and our shared life together stopped.

Much like my conversation with Dr. Biles about a cesarean section so many years earlier, I stared blankly at the telephone that conveyed words I did not wish to hear.

Silence ensued on both ends of the telephone. Eventually I managed to say, "That's okay, honey. Thanks for all you did." But even as we spoke, Frodo's death really wasn't sinking in; it didn't seem real. No way that after this determined effort, I fell short of reaching her just hours before she passed away. This seemed like the bad dream of a weary traveler.

But it wasn't a dream.

Frodo died without me.

After staying on the phone for a time, with really nothing left to say, we said good-bye amidst my promise to rest up before continuing the rest of the way to Maine.

I sat down on the bed of the Kingsville Motel, saddened, stunned, and all alone, the rain pounding down outside. Despite the overwhelming fatigue, one final bit of clarity crept into my mind. I thought back to the improbable start of a young man and a pregnant cat that needed one another desperately at the time their lives intersected. I thought about more than a decade of laughing and loving and spoiling rotten. Of relocations and pigeons and Christmas trees in the living room. I mused about Tide baths and head bobbing, a cat enema at home, so many great vets over the years, and a lifetime of a mother cat with her son. And yes, I thought about how all of it unceremoniously crashed, with me unable to do a damn thing about it.

Physically and mentally exhausted, sitting on the edge of a bed in a cheap motel room in North Kingsville, Ohio, I was left with nothing of Frodo but her imprint on my heart.

* * *

Donna and I had completely different experiences during those few days. I was initially oblivious to the problem, then fretting and frozen with indecision, and then desperate to return speedily to Maine. Donna witnessed the steep decline, did everything she could to reverse the tide, and then watched helplessly as Frodo slipped away.

Despite Donna's worries, deep down I always believed that Frodo would make it until I was there to hold her in my arms that final time. We had traveled so very far together—too far for things to end this way. No way that she would die just short of me arriving home. I never believed that would happen.

But it did. Later on, I asked Donna over and over what transpired in the final hours, so that I could reconcile the prognosis of at least ten more days with the reality of her death within hours. Not much of a story, as it turned out. Frodo's breathing gradually grew shallower, and her pulse started dropping. Bringing her back into the office would cause yet another setback that would probably kill her, the vet advised Donna. Time to let her go.

Perhaps hearing my voice had somehow given Frodo permission to give up the fight.

Donna said she pulled my little white princess out of the oxygen tent in her waning moments of life and placed her atop my terrycloth bathrobe on our basement couch. Out of breath, out of energy, out of life, and for three weeks out of touch with the man she adored, Frodo heaved a final sigh and quietly died in the arms of the other woman.

Satisfaction came from knowing that Frodo died in her home and in a natural way, rather than at a vet's office. She passed from this life close to the woodstove where she toasted herself on cold winter nights. And it was comforting to know that Donna and Brandy were there with her and that she was enveloped in the warmth and scent of my bathrobe. She died as we all should and hope we will, quietly in the arms of our loved ones.

My whole professional life has been spent as a wordsmith, but I can craft no phrase that conveys my sadness that night.

* * *

So much, I longed to say a proper good-bye. I thought then, and sometimes think even now, about whether Frodo was thinking about me during her final days, wondering where in the world I was, or why I had left as her life wound down. Always I had been at her side.

Bless her always-thoughtful heart, Mom had secretly packed a few Frodo photos along with provisions in the car, perhaps as inspiration to keep me going. As I sat in my North Kingsville hotel room, I looked wistfully at those photos.

I rested fitfully for a couple of hours until the sun started to rise. The soaking rain had dissipated, and the rest had helped me regain my wits. There was nothing more to do for my now departed friend, but at least I could head home to Donna. Sitting alone in the Kingsville Motel for any length of time suddenly seemed stupid. So only a few hours after waking up the grumpy hotel lady, I packed my bags. Mom of the mom-and-pop motel surely wondered what I was all about.

Before leaving the room, I took a final look around. So many in this world have faced so much worse than a healthy man losing a beautiful cat who had lived a wonderful life, but this was the place where I heard my sad news, so it seemed as though I should take stock of the surroundings, sort of like Frodo did the first day she walked into my apartment. I grabbed the business card of the Kingsville Motel sitting in my room and stuck it in my pocket.

Twelve years had passed since Frodo had first appeared on my steps.

I drove the remaining miles home the next day, but without the same reckless abandon. Stopping periodically for gas and coffee, and to walk off some of the stiffness in my back, I arrived home in the evening, just one day before my birthday. For the first time since that day on the steps of the Ashley Square apartments, I was not met at the door with a rubby.

14

Smuggling Plans

FOR A LONG TIME to follow, I would sit in the mornings on the rose-colored La-Z-Boy recliner that sat closest to the living-room picture window. That particular chair had been a hub of household activity for years. It was the perfect spot to read the morning paper. If you were a cat, the perfect piece of furniture from which to try for that ever-elusive spider plant hanging from the ceiling, purposely placed just out of a cat's reach. A great chair to sleep on in winter, and if you were a white cat, to lie contently upon your man's long legs and soak up the heat from that wonderful fireplace with the built-in hot-air blowers.

Just outside the window were two maple trees in our front yard. In winter, Frodo lay on any barren spot of our black asphalt driveway for warmth, but in the summer she usually toasted herself on the driveway for just a little while before moving under the shade of those maple trees to cool down.

Her routine was the cat equivalent of soaking in the hot tub, followed by a cold swim.

When Civil War history was in vogue, in the days of Ken Burns's documentary series on PBS, one would hear the possibly apocryphal words surrounding the death of Confederate general Thomas "Stonewall" Jackson, who died after he was accidentally shot by one of his soldiers. "Let us cross over the river," he reportedly said as he lay abed in his dying moments, "and rest under the shade of the trees."

Sipping my coffee and reading the *Bangor Daily News* each morning, I sat in the La-Z-Boy and looked at the maple trees, wondering if somewhere out there Frodo was resting comfortably in the shade.

When Donna couldn't reach me that night as I was racing through Ohio in the New Yorker, she called my parents. Right after hearing that Frodo had died, my Lutheran mother sat down and penned me a short note, touching for its utter honesty. She shared her memories of Frodo and then wrote in part, "I don't know much about kitty heaven, but if there is one, I'm sure that Frodo is there, still being the princess she has always been."

It was in this note that Mom also shared her belief that Frodo was sent by a guardian angel to salve my spirit at a difficult time in my life.

Comforting was the fact that Frodo led the ultimate cat life. She started out as a pregnant stray with a limp, but she found a home and lived a reasonably long life full of material comfort, constant companionship, and love. She died peacefully and quietly at home, nestled in the clothing of the man she loved.

* * *

Donna's efforts to cushion Frodo's death touched me, for it was her loss too. When I pulled into the driveway with the New Yorker, exhausted and sorrowful, she came outside to greet me. She silently hugged me for several unhurried minutes.

She led me up the stairs Frodo had climbed so many times. Sitting by the fireplace were fresh-cut flowers, hastily scribbled cards, and an artist's painting of Frodo that Donna had commissioned one year as a Christmas present; it still hangs on a bedroom wall. Perhaps unexpectedly, I found comfort in the words jotted down in the cards from my Maine friends and neighbors. They all conveyed the simple message that Frodo's cat life mattered so much precisely because it mattered so much to me.

Donna did other thoughtful things to ease the pain. Old-time rock-and-rollers will recall Dr. Hook & the Medicine Show, the band that sang mostly booze and flirty tunes, but also penned a favorite song of mine whose line was this: "You are my one true friend, always my one true friend." Donna found a cat card with a verse that read, "You will always be my best friend." She penned in Frodo's name, replete with little paw prints. She bought expensive champagne and affixed two little white kitties to matching glasses. The next time we headed over to our Acadia National Park stomping grounds, we drank a toast to the deceased princess. We did so as the beautiful sun dropped behind the mountains at our backs and the icy waters of the North Atlantic lapped at our feet. We did so with laughs rather than tears, at the thought of toasting the life of a cat.

Later on, Donna printed a postcard of my favorite Frodo photo with a beautiful verse. She also handed me an album of favorite pictures. And she bought me a pewter pencil holder for my office, with photos of Frodo encased on all four sides. It's still in use.

These objects didn't replace Frodo, but they weren't intended to do so.

I remembered her in my own unique way. When I licensed the New Yorker in Maine, in those days before blockbuster movies about hobbits, I sprung for the vanity plate "Frodo." The Frodomobile, as Donna and I referred to the New Yorker, drew a good many chuckles from literature-savvy Mainers in places like Orono and Camden.

Eventually, State Farm Insurance came to own the Frodomobile, the result of Donna's unfortunate smack into the back of a small truck. But the Frodo license plate survived the crash. And I transferred it to my next vehicle—another Pontiac Bonneville—as allowed by Maine law.

AMC Gremlins were no longer for sale.

* * *

Events conspired to make things worse at the bitter end. Frodo was cremated on my actual birthday, and odd circumstances involving the crematorium meant that we picked up her ashes two days later, on Donna's actual birthday.

And yet I've always been comforted by the fact that we did everything possible for Frodo while she was alive, and that she enjoyed her life with us. A final anecdote provides proof. Donna threw a Christmas party at our house for fellow hospital workers. As people chatted away in the living room for what turned out to be Frodo's last Christmas, she gleefully jumped on top of a chair and then the table in the dining room, helping herself to a platter of meats and cheeses. Too late to stop the crime, the visitors watched the criminal in action as she munched on their food.

And now all these many years later, I still have the ashes of the little white kitty in my possession. I am planning to have those ashes go in sometime and somewhere with me. Why, you might ask? I figure it this way: if it turns out that there is not some kitty heaven, I'll do just like I did at that economy hotel in Topeka. I'll sneak Frodo in with me.

Think of it as a final, non-stop rubby.